CRITICAL REASONING & READING COMPREHENSION

Verbal Preparation Guide

This unique guide illustrates how to deconstruct arguments and reading passages using innovative diagramming techniques designed to build speed and improve accuracy. Understanding the underlying structures of arguments and passages is the key to quick reading and precise analysis.

Critical Reasoning and Reading Comprehension GMAT Preparation Guide

10-digit International Standard Book Number: 0-9748069-6-X
13-digit International Standard Book Number: 978-0-9748069-6-9

Note: *GMAT, Graduate Management Admission Test, Graduate Management
Admission Council,* and *GMAC* are all registered trademarks of the Graduate
Management Admission Council which neither sponsors nor is affiliated in any way
with this product.

7 GUIDE INSTRUCTIONAL SERIES

Math GMAT Preparation Guides

Number Properties (ISBN: 0-9748069-0-0)

FDP's: Fractions, Decimals, & Percents (ISBN: 0-9748069-1-9)

Equations, Inequalities, & VIC's (ISBN: 0-9748069-3-5)

Word Translations (ISBN: 0-9748069-2-7)

Geometry (ISBN: 0-9748069-4-3)

Verbal GMAT Preparation Guides

Critical Reasoning & Reading Comprehension (ISBN: 0-9748069-6-X)

Sentence Correction (ISBN: 0-9748069-5-1)

HOW OUR GMAT PREP BOOKS ARE DIFFERENT

One of our core beliefs at Manhattan GMAT is that a curriculum should be more than just a guidebook of tricks and tips. Scoring well on the GMAT requires a curriculum that builds true content knowledge and understanding. Skim through this guide and this is what you will see:

You will *not* find page after page of guessing techniques.

Instead, you will find a highly organized and structured guide that actually teaches you the content you need to know to do well on the GMAT.

You *will* find many more pages-per-topic than in all-in-one tomes.

Each chapter covers one specific topic area in-depth, explaining key concepts, detailing in-depth strategies, and building specific skills through Manhattan GMAT's *In-Action* problem sets (with comprehensive explanations). Why are there 7 guides? Each of the 7 books (5 Math, 2 Verbal) covers a major content area in extensive depth, allowing you to delve deep into each topic. In addition, you may purchase only those guides that pertain to your weaknesses.

This guide is challenging - it asks you to do more, not less.

It starts with the fundamental skills, but does not end there; it also includes the *most advanced content* that many other prep books ignore. As the average GMAT score required to gain admission to top business schools continues to rise, this guide, together with the simulated online practice exams and bonus question bank included with your purchase, provides test-takers with the depth and volume of advanced material essential for succeeding on the GMAT's computer adaptive format.

This guide is ambitious - developing mastery is its goal.

Developed by Manhattan GMAT's staff of REAL teachers (all of whom have 99th percentile official GMAT scores), our ambitious curriculum seeks to provide test-takers of all levels with an in-depth and carefully tailored approach that enables our students to achieve mastery. If you are looking to learn more than just the "process of elimination" and if you want to develop skills, strategies, and a confident approach to any problem that you may see on the GMAT, then our sophisticated preparation guides are the tools to get you there.

HOW TO ACCESS YOUR ONLINE RESOURCES

Please read this entire page of information, all the way down to the bottom of the page! This page describes WHAT online resources are included with the purchase of this book and HOW to access these resources.

[**If you are a registered Manhattan GMAT student** and have received this book as part of your course materials, you have AUTOMATIC access to ALL of our online resources. This includes all simulated practice exams, question banks, and online updates to this book. To access these resources, follow the instructions in the Welcome Guide provided to you at the start of your program. Do NOT follow the instructions below.]

If you have purchased this book, your purchase includes 1 YEAR OF ONLINE ACCESS to the following:

> **3 Simulated Online Practice Exams**

> **Bonus Online Question Bank for CRITICAL REASONING & READING COMP**

> **Online Updates to the Content in this Book**

The 3 full-length practice exams included with the purchase of this book are delivered online using Manhattan GMAT's proprietary online test engine. All questions included in the exams are unique questions written by Manhattan GMAT's expert instructors, all of whom have scored in the 99th percentile on the Official GMAT. The exams are non-adaptive and include questions of varying difficulty levels. At the end of each exam you will receive a score, an analysis of your results, and the opportunity to review detailed explanations for each question. You may choose to take the exams timed or untimed.

The Bonus Online Question Bank for Critical Reasoning & Reading Comp consists of 25 extra practice questions (with detailed explanations) that test the variety of Reasoning & Comprehension skills covered in this book. These questions provide you with extra practice *beyond* the problem sets contained in this book. You may use our online timer to practice your pacing by setting time limits for each question in the bank.

The content contained in this book is updated periodically to ensure that it reflects the GMAT's most current trends. All updated information, including any known errors or changes to this book, is posted online. You will be able to view all updates to this book upon registering for your online access.

Important Note: The 3 online exams included with the purchase of this book are the SAME exams that you receive upon purchasing ANY book in Manhattan GMAT's 7 Book Preparation Series. (See the bottom front cover of this book for a list of all 7 titles.) On the other hand, the Bonus Online Question Bank for CRITICAL REASONING & READING COMPREHENSION is a unique resource that you receive ONLY with the purchase of this specific title.

To access the online resources listed above, you will need this book in front of you and you will need to register your information online. This book includes access to the above resources for ONE PERSON ONLY.

To register and start using your online resources, please go online to the following URL:

http://www.manhattangmat.com/access.cfm   (Double check that you have typed this in accurately!)

Your 1 year of online access begins on the day that you register at the above URL.

CRITICAL REASONING

TABLE OF CONTENTS

g

READING COMPREHENSION

g | Critical Reasoning

Chapter 1
of
CRITICAL REASONING &
READING COMPREHENSION

ARGUMENT
STRUCTURE

In This Chapter . . .

- Identify the Parts of an Argument
- Signal Words for Argument Parts
- Real Arguments: Identifying Premises and Conclusions
- Real Arguments: Not all the Same
- Conclusion in the Question
- 2 Conclusions: Internal vs. External

ARGUMENT STRUCTURE

The Critical Reasoning section of the GMAT involves reading brief arguments (each argument is generally one to three sentences long) and answering questions relating to those arguments.

In order to analyze GMAT arguments, it is important to understand their basic structure:

(Assumptions) + Premises = Conclusion

In words, assumptions and premises lead to a conclusion.

ASSUMPTIONS are UNSTATED parts of the argument that are necessary to reach the given conclusion. In the formula above, the word **Assumptions** is put in parentheses to signal that assumptions are NEVER stated in the written argument.

PREMISES are STATED pieces of information or evidence that are necessary to reach the given conclusion.

The main point of the argument is the CONCLUSION, which is logically supported by the assumptions and premises.

Think of the conclusion as the top of a building, supported by the building itself (the premises) and the unseen underground foundation (the assumptions).

Assumptions are never stated in the argument.

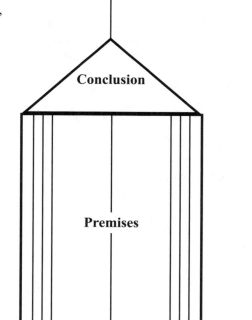

Manhattan**GMAT***Prep
the new standard

Identify the Parts of an Argument

In order to do well on GMAT Critical Reasoning questions, it is essential to be able to identify quickly the parts of an argument. Consider the following argument:

> **Studying regularly is one factor that has been shown to improve one's performance on the GMAT. Melissa took the GMAT and scored a 500. If she studies several times a week, Melissa can expect to improve her score.**

In analyzing an argument, you should first look for the conclusion, which is the main point of the argument. The conclusion is often the last sentence of an argument, but not always. Sometimes the conclusion appears as the first sentence.

Where is the CONCLUSION? The main point of this argument is the last sentence:

> **If she studies several times a week, Melissa can expect to improve her score.**

After finding the conclusion, look for the premises that lead to the conclusion. Premises include ALL the pieces of information in the argument (except the conclusion). Premises provide evidence that supports, or leads to, the conclusion.

Where are the PREMISES? Since everything except the conclusion is considered a premise, each of the first two sentences is a premise.

> Premise: **Studying regularly is one factor that has been shown to improve one's performance on the GMAT.**
> Premise: **Melissa took the GMAT and scored a 500.**

Usually, all you will need to find are the conclusion and the premises. Sometimes, however, the GMAT will ask you to identify an assumption.

Where are the ASSUMPTIONS? Assumptions are unstated parts of the argument. Therefore, you will NEVER find an assumption stated in an argument. However, assumptions are necessary to reach the given conclusion. One assumption in this argument is that studying several times a week qualifies as studying regularly.

Premises present facts that support the conclusion of the argument.

Signal Words for Argument Parts

One way to recognize the conclusion of an argument is by looking out for certain "signal words" that often precede a conclusion.

The most common conclusion signals on the GMAT are:

Therefore	**So**
As a result	**Consequently**
Suggests	**Thus**
Indicates	**Hence**
Accordingly	**It follows that**

Conclusions are also signaled by their strong tone, often marked by words such as **should** ("This law **should** be enacted . . .").

Premises can also be recognized by certain "signal words." The most common premise signals on the GMAT are:

Since	**Because**
Due to	**Given that**

In order to separate the conclusion from the premises, look for the last deduction made in the argument. The deduction that takes place last (chronologically) is always the conclusion. (This does not necessarily mean that the conclusion will appear last in the passage.)

The conclusion happens last in time, but does not necessarily appear last in the text of the argument.

Real Arguments: Identifying Premises and Conclusions

The best way to understand the structure of GMAT arguments is to practice reading a particular argument, identifying each point as either a premise or the conclusion.

The following examples use arguments taken from real past GMAT exams. These arguments can be found in *The Official Guide for GMAT Review, 11th Edition* or *The Official Guide for GMAT Verbal Review.*

> **A program instituted in a particular state allows parents to prepay their children's future college tuition at current rates. The program then pays the tuition annually for the child at any of the state's public colleges in which the child enrolls. Parents should participate in the program as a means of decreasing the cost of their children's college education.**

The Official Guide for GMAT Verbal Review, #29
GMAT® *questions are the property of the Graduate Management Admission Council*® *and are reprinted with its permission.*

This argument consists of three sentences:

The CONCLUSION of this argument is the last sentence, because this is the main point of the argument. Notice its strong tone through the use of the word **should**.

The first two sentences are therefore PREMISES. Notice that, in this argument, the premises are both facts.

> **The proposal to hire ten new police officers in Middletown is quite foolish. There is sufficient funding to pay the salaries of the new officers, but not the salaries of additional court and prison employees to process the increased caseload of arrests and convictions that new officers usually generate.**

The Official Guide for GMAT Review (11th edition), #120
GMAT® *questions are the property of the Graduate Management Admission Council*® *and are reprinted with its permission.*

This argument consists of two sentences:

The CONCLUSION of this argument is the first sentence, because this is the main point of the argument. Notice its strong tone through the use of the phrase **quite foolish**.

The second sentence contains several PREMISES, which provide important information.

The conclusion is the main point the speaker is trying to argue. Therefore, the conclusion should be *arguable* either way.

Real Arguments: Not all the Same

Not all GMAT arguments can be neatly broken down by sentence into premises and conclusions. Some arguments have a slightly different structure. Consider the following example:

> **Kale has more nutritional value than spinach. But since collard greens have more nutritional value than lettuce, it follows that kale has more nutritional value than lettuce.**
>
> *The Official Guide for GMAT Review (11th edition), #107*
> *GMAT® questions are the property of the Graduate Management*
> *Admission Council® and are reprinted with its permission.*

This argument consists of two sentences:

The CONCLUSION of this argument is the last part of the second sentence: **it follows that kale has more nutritional value than lettuce**. Notice the conclusion is signaled by the phrase **it follows that**.

The rest of this passage consists of PREMISES. The first sentence is a premise that presents information relating kale to spinach. The first part of the second sentence is a premise that gives information relating collard greens to lettuce.

This example illustrates that a premise and a conclusion can appear together in the same sentence.

Now consider an example that contains NO conclusion:

> **Increases in the level of high-density lipoprotein (HDL) in the human bloodstream lower bloodstream-cholesterol levels by increasing the body's capacity to rid itself of excess cholesterol. Levels of HDL in the bloodstream of some individuals are significantly increased by a program of regular exercise and weight reduction.**
>
> *The Official Guide for GMAT Verbal Review, #2*
> *GMAT® questions are the property of the Graduate Management*
> *Admission Council® and are reprinted with its permission.*

This argument consists of two sentences:

Both sentences present factual information; neither presents a compelling main point or claim. Thus, this is an argument that consists of several PREMISES but no real CONCLUSION.

Many GMAT critical reasoning questions ask you to draw a conclusion, make an inference, or explain a situation (chosen from a set of answer choices) based solely on a passage of premises.

Not all GMAT arguments have a stated conclusion. Sometimes the conclusion is in the answer choices.

Conclusion in the Question

Sometimes the conclusion of a particular argument is not in the passage itself, but instead can be found in the question that follows the passage. Consider the following example:

> **Firms adopting "profit-related-pay" (PRP) contracts pay wages at levels that vary with the firm's profits. In the metalworking industry last year, firms with PRP contracts in place showed productivity per worker on average 13 percent higher than that of their competitors who used more traditional contracts.**
>
> **If, on the basis of the evidence above, it is argued that PRP contracts increase worker productivity, which of the following, if true, would most seriously weaken that argument?**

> *The Official Guide for GMAT Review (11th edition), #118*
>
> *GMAT® questions are the property of the Graduate Management Admission Council® and are reprinted with its permission.*

If the language of the question is specific to the argument, look for the conclusion there.

Notice that the passage itself consists of two sentences, which are both PREMISES. The first premise explains the term **PRP**. The second premise gives statistical information about PRP usage in the metalworking industry.

The CONCLUSION of this argument is given in the question: **PRP contracts increase worker productivity**. This is the main point of the argument. (The question goes on to ask for a way to weaken the argument.)

2 Conclusions: Internal vs. External

Sometimes a passage contains TWO conclusions that are opposed to one another. The first conclusion is inside the passage itself—termed the **internal** conclusion. The second conclusion is found in the question. This second conclusion—termed the **external** conclusion—makes its own assessment (usually a negative assessment) of the first conclusion. Take a look at the following example:

> **A certain mayor has proposed a fee of five dollars per day on private vehicles entering the city, claiming that the fee will alleviate the city's traffic congestion. The mayor reasons that, since the fee will exceed the cost of round-trip bus fare from many nearby points, many people will switch from using their cars to using the bus.**
>
> **Which of the following statements, if true, provides the best evidence that the mayor's reasoning is flawed?**
>
> *The Official Guide for GMAT Verbal Review, #39*
> GMAT® questions are the property of the Graduate Management
> Admission Council® and are reprinted with its permission.

Some passages have both an internal conclusion and an external conclusion.

The passage focuses on the mayor's proposal to institute a five dollar daily fee on private vehicles entering the city. The mayor's conclusion is found in the first sentence: **the fee will alleviate the city's traffic congestion.**

The second sentence consists of premises leading up to this conclusion. One premise is the fact that **the fee will exceed the cost of round-trip bus fare from many nearby points.** Another premise is the mayor's claim that **people will switch from using their cars to using the bus.** Note that this claim is not considered the conclusion, because it is not the mayor's final claim. Rather, this claim *leads* to the mayor's ultimate conclusion that the fee will alleviate the city's traffic congestion.

When we move on to the question that follows the argument, we see that the question makes its own assessment of the mayor's conclusion. The question asks for evidence that **the mayor's reasoning is flawed.** This is an external conclusion—a statement that assesses (negatively, in this case) the conclusion made by the mayor.

Thus, we have an example of a passage that has two competing conclusions. The internal conclusion, found in the argument, is the mayor's ultimate point. The external conclusion, found in the question, is a claim that *comments on* the mayor's conclusion.

Critical Reasoning

Now that you have completed your study of ARGUMENT STRUCTURE, it is time to test your skills on passages that have actually appeared on real GMAT exams over the past several years.

The problem set that follows is composed of 20 Critical Reasoning passages from two books published by GMAC (Graduate Management Admission Council):

The Official Guide for GMAT Review, 11th Edition (pages 468-504)
The Official Guide for GMAT Verbal Review (pages 116-142)

The passages below exhibit a representative sampling of ARGUMENT STRUCTURES. For each passage, complete the following in a notebook:

(1)   Find and write out the conclusion of the passage. Be sure to check both the argument and the question, as occasionally the conclusion can be found in the question. Also, be aware that some passages have both an internal and an external conclusion.

(2)   If the passage does not include a conclusion, indicate this with the words **no given conclusion**.

Note that you are not actually answering these questions! You are only identifying the conclusion of each argument. In subsequent problem sets, you will be answering these questions. For now, however, concentrate only on identifying the conclusion.

The answers to the 20 passages in this exercise can be found on the following page.

Find the Conclusion
> *11th Edition:* 3, 18, 34, 56, 64, 65, 67, 73, 78, 79, 102
> *Verbal Review:* 3, 6, 27, 36, 53, 57, 61, 71, 77

11th Edition:

3. Conclusion: Third sentence: **Thus, in those days . . . prime of life.**

18. Conclusion: Second sentence: **As a result . . . a seat belt.**

34. **No given conclusion**

56. **No given conclusion**

64. Conclusion: End of second sentence: **any fever that . . . the malarial parasite.**

65. Conclusion: First sentence: **Most consumers do . . . equipment they purchase.**

67. Conclusion: Second sentence: **Therefore, the citizens . . . of Town T.**

73. Internal Conclusion: Second sentence: **To attract students to physics . . . visual images.**
    External Conclusion: Part of the question: **proposed curriculum will be successful . . . students.**

78. Conclusion: Second sentence: **Therefore, replacement of . . . of typing costs.**

79. Conclusion: First sentence: **An overly centralized . . . came to power.**

102. Conclusion: Second sentence: **If a newlywed . . . remained in Louisiana.**

Verbal Review:

3. Conclusion: First sentence: **A cost-effective . . . 500 miles apart.**

6. Conclusion: Third sentence: **Obviously, the mayor's publicity . . . bus to work.**

27. Conclusion: End of third sentence: **so some alarm boxes are still necessary.**

36. Conclusion: End of second sentence: **scientists have . . . the reproductive cycle.**

53. Conclusion: Part of the Question: **To support a . . . surgical procedures.**

57. **No given conclusion**

61. **No given conclusion**

71. Internal Conclusion: Middle of the first sentence: ***Home Dec . . .* plans to maximize its profits.**
    External Conclusion: Part of the Question: **profits are likely to decline if the plan is instituted.**

77. **No given conclusion**

Chapter 2
of
CRITICAL REASONING & READING COMPREHENSION

DIAGRAMMING

In This Chapter . . .

DIAGRAMMING

The most effective way to improve your Critical Reasoning performance on tough problems is to DIAGRAM the argument. The diagramming strategy works for several reasons:

(1) Diagramming <u>SAVES</u> time: Critical Reasoning arguments are short but complex. They are almost always between one and three sentences long. However, reading an argument once is generally not sufficient to understand it. Rereading the argument several times adds little to understanding, while taking up valuable time. On the other hand, diagramming an argument on the first reading makes it readily understandable and eliminates time spent on repeated rereading.

(2) Diagramming <u>CATCHES</u> key details: Many Critical Reasoning arguments hinge on key details. These details are designed to escape your notice during reading. On the other hand, diagramming helps to highlight the key details of an argument. Translating a passage into a diagram forces you to notice and evaluate details.

(3) Diagramming <u>FOCUSES</u> on argument structure: The questions which the GMAT asks about Critical Reasoning passages are almost always related to one of the structural parts of the argument: the premises, the conclusion, or the hidden assumptions. Diagramming involves identifying the structural parts of each argument. Since a question generally asks about one part of an argument, a diagram allows you to focus your attention on that specific element.

Diagramming can help you identify the conclusion of the argument.

How to Diagram an Argument

Diagramming an argument is a simple process that involves translating a passage that you read into something visual that you write. The form of the diagram is NOT essential; it is the act of writing that matters, as it dramatically increases your understanding of the argument. Several principles should guide your diagram:

(1)   Go sentence by sentence. Read one sentence and then rewrite it. Read the next sentence and then rewrite that. DO NOT read the whole passage through once and then begin rewriting. This wastes valuable time.

(2)   A diagram is a LIST, not an elaborate drawing. A good diagram consists of a passage rewritten as a list of brief informative points. Each point gets its own line. Though not necessary for an effective diagram, drawings can be used to illustrate the structure of an argument. For example, some arguments can be effectively diagrammed by placing each point on a timeline or in a comparison chart.

(3)   Rewriting a point does not mean putting it in your own words. When you are rewriting a passage, your goal is to make each point brief. This means eliminating unnecessary words. It does not mean changing important words by paraphrasing them. Feel free to keep the EXACT key wording of the points. Paraphrasing, while sometimes helpful, can also unintentionally eliminate important details.

(4)   Underline key words and details. As you are writing each point, underline any words or details that you think may be key to the argument. In particular, be sure to underline 'boundary words,' which will be discussed later.

(5)   Use arrows for cause and effect. Cause and effect comes up frequently in arguments. Use an arrow to signal that one event causes another event.

(6)   If an argument contains speakers or dates, keep them organized by placing them before a given point with a colon (e.g. **Martha: The GMAT is easy because** ...).

(7)   Label each point in your list as either a premise (P) or the conclusion (C). This is the key to your diagram. Each point MUST be assigned either the letter P or the letter C.

(8)   Number the premises in a logical order, either chronologically or by cause and effect. It is essential that you order the premises, so that you can fully understand the structure and logic of the argument, identify the conclusion, and evaluate potential flaws and assumptions. After you number the premises, assign the last number to the conclusion, since the conclusion is the final point in the argument.

Include all numbers and statistics in your diagram.

Diagramming Real Arguments

Diagramming is a powerful strategy that is best learned by repeated practice with REAL GMAT arguments. The following examples provide model diagrams for arguments taken from real past GMAT exams. These arguments are the same ones used as examples in the previous section covering argument structure. Now, instead of simply analyzing the structure of each passage, we will actually diagram each passage.

All of the following examples use arguments taken from *The Official Guide for GMAT Review, 11th Edition* or *The Official Guide for GMAT Verbal Review*.

> **A program instituted in a particular state allows parents to prepay their children's future college tuition at current rates. The program then pays the tuition annually for the child at any of the state's public colleges in which the child enrolls. Parents should participate in the program as a means of decreasing the cost of their children's college education.**

The Official Guide for GMAT Verbal Review, #29
GMAT® *questions are the property of the Graduate Management Admission Council® and are reprinted with its permission.*

(1) P Program: Parents <u>prepay</u> children's future college tuition at <u>current rates</u>

(2) P Program will pay tuition for child at <u>any state public college</u>

(3) C Parents <u>should</u> participate <u>to decrease cost</u> of children's college ed

This diagram is a list of three points. The first two are premises, labeled with the letter P. The third point is the conclusion, labeled with the letter C. Each point uses essentially the same wording as that of the original passage. The only change is that the points eliminate unnecessary words from the passage, and some use abbreviations.

Notice that key words and details are underlined. In particular, the specific boundary of the program—**any state public college**—is underlined. The specific reason given in the conclusion—**to decrease cost**—is underlined as well.

Also notice that the points are numbered in a logical order. FIRST, parents prepay tuition; only THEN will the program pay for the child to attend a state public college. THEREFORE, these things being true, parents should participate. Note that the conclusion should always be numbered last.

> Identify each point as either a premise or a conclusion.

Reorder When Needed

Often, the logical order of the premises is different from the order in which they appear in the text. When this is the case, you can write them as they appear in the text and then number them more logically afterwards.

Consider the argument below:

> **The proposal to hire ten new police officers in Middletown is quite foolish. There is sufficient funding to pay the salaries of the new officers, but not the salaries of additional court and prison employees to process the increased caseload of arrests and convictions that new officers usually generate.**

The Official Guide for GMAT Review (11th edition), #120
GMAT® questions are the property of the Graduate Management
Admission Council® and are reprinted with its permission.

(4) C Middletown Proposal to hire 10 new police officers is <u>foolish</u>

(1) P There <u>is</u> funding for new <u>officers</u>

(3) P There is <u>not</u> funding for <u>additional workers</u> needed for <u>bigger caseload</u>

(2) P New officers <u>usually</u> generate <u>increased</u> caseload of <u>arrests and convictions</u>

Notice that the second sentence has been divided into 3 points (all premises). The key to successful diagramming is giving each point its own line. Assign numbers to rearrange the order of the points logically, always ending with the conclusion.

Words like THEREFORE, HOWEVER, AND, and BUT can help you logically order the argument and identify the conclusion. You will also be able to locate gaps in the argument. **There is funding for new officers**; HOWEVER, **these new officers will generate an increased caseload**, AND **there is not funding for additional workers to process this increased caseload**. THEREFORE, **the proposal is foolish**. Even though the conclusion is the first sentence in the passage, it is numbered last, since it hinges upon the logic provided in the premises.

When you diagram on the GMAT, you do not need to rewrite the points in order. Simply assigning them numbers will help you to make sense of the chronology or logical order.

Conclusion in the Question

Sometimes, the conclusion of the argument is in the question itself. When the language of the question is specific to the situation described in the argument, this can often be a clue that the conclusion is in the question.

Consider this argument:

> **Firms adopting "profit-related-pay" (PRP) contracts pay wages at levels that vary with the firm's profits. In the metalworking industry last year, firms with PRP contracts in place showed productivity per worker on average 13 percent higher than that of their competitors who used more traditional contracts.**
>
> **If, on the basis of the evidence above, it is argued that PRP contracts increase worker productivity, which of the following, if true, would most seriously weaken that argument?**

> *The Official Guide for GMAT Review (11th edition), #118*
> *GMAT® questions are the property of the Graduate Management*
> *Admission Council® and are reprinted with its permission.*

(1) P Firms adopting PRP contracts pay <u>wages</u> that <u>vary</u> with <u>firm's profits</u>

(2) P <u>Metal</u>: PRP firms showed <u>13% higher</u> worker <u>productivity</u> vs. non-PRP firms

(3) C PRP contracts <u>increase</u> worker <u>productivity</u>

Notice how the question contains language such as **PRP contracts** and **worker productivity**. This should indicate to you that the conclusion may be contained within the question. Be sure to include the conclusion in your diagram even when it is located in the question.

Be sure to include all the key details in your diagram.

Arguments with No Conclusion

The conclusion of the argument is not always present. Sometimes, you are asked to select the correct conclusion from among the answer choices. In these arguments, simply diagram the premises. This will make it easier for you to identify the conclusion later.

Consider this argument:

> **Increases in the level of high-density lipoprotein (HDL) in the human bloodstream lower bloodstream-cholesterol levels by increasing the body's capacity to rid itself of excess cholesterol. Levels of HDL in the bloodstream of some individuals are significantly increased by a program of regular exercise and weight reduction.**
>
> *The Official Guide for GMAT Verbal Review, #2*
> *GMAT® questions are the property of the Graduate Management Admission Council® and are reprinted with its permission.*

(3) P <u>Increase</u> in level of <u>HDL</u> in blood → <u>lowers</u> blood <u>cholesterol</u>

(2) P HDL <u>increases</u> body's capacity to get rid of excess cholesterol

(1) P <u>Regular exercise + weight reduction</u> → <u>increase</u> HDL level in <u>some</u> people

Note that this passage consists solely of premises without a conclusion. All of the points are statements of fact; none are arguable. No claim seems to be made at all. Notice, as well, that the arrow is used as a quick way to show that one event causes another event. Finally, notice that the word **some** is underlined, as it provides an important boundary for that premise.

We have reordered these premises by assigning numbers to the them. Exercise and weight reduction increase the levels of HDL in some people. This is significant because HDL helps the body get rid of cholesterol. Therefore, increased HDL lowers a person's cholesterol. Ordering the premises in the argument will help us to identify the logical conclusion from among the five answer choices.

Faulty Reasoning

As you diagram, you may notice flaws in the argument structure. For example, the premises may not lead directly to the conclusion, or there may be a clear gap in the reasoning. This is something that the GMAT question relating to this argument will address. It is not something you should worry about in your diagram. The purpose of the diagram is simply to list (not evaluate) the given information.

Consider this argument:

> **Kale has more nutritional value than spinach. But since collard greens have more nutritional value than lettuce, it follows that kale has more nutritional value than lettuce.**
>
> *The Official Guide for GMAT Review (11th edition), #107*
> *GMAT® questions are the property of the Graduate Management*
> *Admission Council® and are reprinted with its permission.*

(1) P kale > spinach

(2) P collard greens > lettuce

(3) C kale > lettuce

In this example, the expression **more nutritional value** has been replaced with the shorthand mathematical symbol >. Notice that the last point—**kale > lettuce**—is labeled as the conclusion because of the signal words **it follows that**.

It seems clear that the two premises in this passage don't necessarily lead to the given conclusion. Diagramming can help you become aware of the flaws in the argument's reasoning, so that you can better answer the question asked about the argument.

Diagramming Internal and External Conclusions

Let's look at a final argument:

> **A certain mayor has proposed a fee of five dollars per day on private vehicles entering the city, claiming that the fee will alleviate the city's traffic congestion. The mayor reasons that, since the fee will exceed the cost of round-trip bus fare from many nearby points, many people will switch from using their cars to using the bus.**
>
> **Which of the following statements, if true, provides the best evidence that the mayor's reasoning is flawed?**
>
> *The Official Guide for GMAT Verbal Review, #39*
> *GMAT® questions are the property of the Graduate Management*
> *Admission Council® and are reprinted with its permission.*

Diagram the argument first; this will help you evaluate the reasoning later.

Here is a diagram for the preceding argument:

(1) P Mayor: Proposed a $5 fee per day on <u>private</u> vehicles <u>entering</u> the city

(4) IC The fee will <u>alleviate</u> the city's traffic congestion

(2) P Fee will exceed the cost of round-trip bus fare from many nearby points

(3) P <u>Many</u> people will switch from using their cars to using the bus

(5) EC The mayor's reasoning is flawed

Number your diagram to make the structure of the argument more clear.

Notice that the words **private** and **entering** are underlined to highlight the boundaries of the mayor's proposal. The fee is only on private vehicles (as opposed to public) and is only assessed when these vehicles enter the city (as opposed to when they exit the city).

The words **alleviate** and **many** are also underlined because they limit the scope of the mayor's claims. The mayor does not claim that the traffic congestion will end *completely*, only that it will be **alleviated.** The mayor does not claim that *everyone* will switch from using their cars to using the bus, only that **many** people will switch.

In assigning numbers to each of the points in the argument, consider the most logical way for the claims to be ordered. One potentially confusing issue here is that the mayor makes two claims. The mayor claims that **the fee will alleviate the city's traffic congestion** and that **many people will switch from using their cars to using the bus**. In trying to determine which of these is the mayor's ultimate claim—the conclusion—consider which of the following orderings is more logical:

The fee will alleviate the city's traffic congestion.
THEREFORE, many people will switch from using their cars to using the bus.

OR

Many people will switch from using their cars to using the bus.
THEREFORE, the fee will alleviate the city's traffic congestion.

Clearly, the second of these two options is more logical. Thus, the mayor's claim that many people will switch from using their cars to using the bus is a premise leading to the mayor's conclusion that the fee will alleviate the city's traffic congestion.

Beyond the mayor's conclusion that **the fee will alleviate the city's traffic congestion**, there is another conclusion that is found in the question that follows the passage. This conclusion makes the assessment that **the mayor's reasoning is flawed**. The mayor's conclusion is labeled **IC** for *internal conclusion*, while the conclusion in the question is labeled **EC** for *external conclusion*.

Critical Reasoning

Now that you have completed your study of DIAGRAMMING, it is time to test your skills on passages that have actually appeared on real GMAT exams over the past several years.

The problem set that follows is composed of 20 Critical Reasoning passages from two books published by GMAC (Graduate Management Admission Council):

The Official Guide for GMAT Review, 11th Edition (pages 468-504)
The Official Guide for GMAT Verbal Review (pages 116-142)

The passages below exhibit a representative sampling of argument structures. These are the same passages used in the previous problem set. Now, however, instead of simply locating the conclusion of the passage, you will be diagramming each passage.

For each passage, complete the following in a notebook:

(1)   Diagram each passage, sentence by sentence, using as guides the diagramming guidelines and model examples given in the previous pages.

(2)   Be sure your diagram is in the form of a list and includes:
          One point per line, labeled as P or C
          Underlined key words (especially details and boundary words)

(3)   Number your listed points in a logical order with the conclusion at the end.

(4)   Time yourself and aim to complete each diagram in approximately 60 to 90 seconds (although your first few diagrams will probably take considerably longer).

Note that you are not actually answering these questions! You are only diagramming them. In subsequent problem sets, you will be answering these questions. For now, however, concentrate only on becoming a diagramming expert.

Although diagrams will vary, model answers to the 20 passages in this problem set can be found on the following pages.

Diagramming
     11th Edition: 3, 18, 34, 56, 64, 65, 67, 73, 78, 79, 102
     Verbal Review: 3, 6, 27, 36, 53, 57, 61, 71, 77

11th Edition:

3:

(1) P Life expectancy: average age at death of live-born population

(2) P Mid-19th cent: life expect in N. Am = 40 yrs

(3) P Now it is nearly 80 yrs

(4) C In those days, people were considered old at age we now consider prime of life

18:

(1) P Opponents of mandatory seat belt laws for drivers and passengers:
    In free society people have right to risks as long as risks don't harm others

(2) C Each person should decide whether or not to wear a seat belt

34:

(1) P Past 3 years: two company divisions performed w/great consistency

(2) P Pharmaceuticals: accounts for 20% dollar sales and 40% profits

(3) P Chemicals: accounts for 80% dollar sales and 60% profits

56:

(2) P Social scientists are underrep on advisory councils of NIH

(1) P Councils advise NIH directors and recommend policy

(3) P Underrep of soc scientists $\rightarrow$ lack of NIH financial support for research in soc sciences

64:

(1) P Red blood cells w/malarial parasite are removed from body after 120 days

(2) P Malarial parasite cannot travel to new gen of red blood cells

(3) C Fever in person more than 120 days after moving to malaria-free region is not due to malarial parasite

65:

(4) C Most consumers do not get much use out of sports equipment they buy

(1) P 17% of US adults own jogging shoes

(2) P Only 45% of j-shoe owners jog more than once/year

(3) P Only 17% of j-shoe owners jog more than once/week

67:

(1) P More newspapers are sold in Town S than sold in Town T

(2) C Town S citizens are better informed re: world events than Town T citizens

73:

(1) P Local board of ed: current phys curric has little relevance to today's world → phys classes attract few h.s. students

(2) IC Board: curric that emphasizes phys principles involved in producing + analyzing visual images will attract students to phys classes

(3) EC Proposed curric will be successful in attracting students

78:

(1) P EFCO keyboard places most used keys nearest typists' strongest fingers

(2) P Result: Faster typing + less fatigue

(3) C Replace standard with EFCO → immediate reduction in typing costs

79:

(3) C Overly centralized economy (not climate changes) → poor agric prod in Country X since new gov came to power

(1) P Neighboring Country Y has experienced same climatic conditions as Country X

(2) P Agric prod in Country Y has been rising

102:

(1) P Average life expectancy for U.S. pop as a whole = 73.9 yrs

(2) P Children born in Hawaii = 77 yr average

(3) P Children born in Louisiana = 71.7 yr average

(4) C If a couple from L has children born in H, the children can expect to live longer than if they were born in L

Verbal Review:

3:

(3) C Cost-effective solution to airport congestion: high speed ground transport between major cities 200-500 miles apart

(1) P Ground transport plan would cost less than expanding airports

(2) P Ground transport plan would reduce # planes clogging airports + airways

6:

(1) P Mayor's bus campaign began 6 months ago

(2) P Since then morning car traffic in midtown has decreased 7%

(3) P Since then, 7% increase in bus riders to midtown

(4) C Mayor has convinced people to take bus (not cars) to work

27:

(1) P Mayor to deactivate city fire alarm boxes since most calls from them are false

(2) P Mayor: most people have access to public/private phones so boxes not needed

(3) P Commercial district has greatest risk of fire, and few res, few public phones

(4) C Editorial: alarm boxes are still necessary

36:

(1) P 20 years after ER Dam was built: none of 8 native species are still reproducing
adequately in river below dam

(2) P Dam reduced range of water temp from 50 to 6

(3) C Scientists: Rising water temp involved in signaling to native species to begin
reproducing

53:

(1) P Great geographical variation in frequency of many surgical procedures

(2) P Variation: up to tenfold per 100,000 in #s of hys, prost, tons

(3) C Much of variation is due to unnecessary surgical procedures

57:

(1) P Meteorite explosion in Siberia had force of 12 MT nuclear blast

(2) P Such explosions in Earth atm occur once per century

(3) P Highly automated computer controlled systems have unpredictable response
to unexpected circumstances

61:

(3) P Tobacco industry is profitable and projections say it will remain so

(1) P In US this year: total amount of tobacco sold by farmers has increased

(2) P In US this year: # of adults who smoke has decreased

71:

(1) P Postage rates are rising

(5) IC HD plans to maximize profits

(2) P HD plans to cut number of issues per year in half

(3) P Quality + number of articles, and subscription price will not change

(4) P Market research: Plan will not affect # of subscribers or advertisers

(6) EC If plan is instituted, HD profits are likely to decline

77:

(1) P Parasitic wasps lay eggs directly into eggs of host

(2) P Wasps lay eggs in exactly right # given the size of host egg

(3) P If too many eggs in host → wasp babies compete to death for food + space

(4) P If too few eggs in host → part of host egg would decay killing wasp babies

Chapter 3
of
CRITICAL REASONING & READING COMPREHENSION

QUESTION TYPES

In This Chapter . . .

- General Strategy: Boundary Words
- General Strategy: Extreme Words
- General Strategy: "Except" Questions
- Type 1: Find an Assumption
- Type 2: Draw a Conclusion
- Type 3: Strengthen the Conclusion: S-W-Slash Chart
- Type 4: Weaken the Conclusion: S-W-Slash Chart
- Type 5: Analyze the Argument Structure
- Minor Question Types

QUESTION TYPES

The final piece of the Critical Reasoning puzzle is the QUESTION that follows the argument. There are several types of questions you can expect on the GMAT.

The 5 major question types are:

(1) Find an Assumption

(2) Draw a Conclusion

(3) Strengthen the Conclusion

(4) Weaken the Conclusion

(5) Analyze the Argument Structure

Familiarize yourself with the major question types.

Notice that three of the five major question types focus on the conclusion. It is clear that the conclusion is the most important part of each argument.

There are also 7 minor question types. They are:

* Explain an Event or Discrepancy
* Make an Inference about a Premise
* Evaluate the Conclusion
* Resolve a Problem

* Provide an Example
* Restate the Conclusion
* Mimic the Argument

General Strategy: Boundary Words

For any question, it is helpful to focus your attention on the boundary words and phrases provided in the argument. These words and phrases narrow the scope of an argument.

Premise: **The percentage of literate adults has increased.**

The boundary word **percentage** limits the scope of the premise. It restricts the meaning to percentage only, as opposed to the actual number of literate adults. (Just because the percentage increased, does not mean that the actual number increased.) The boundary word **adults** also limits the scope of the premise. It restricts the meaning to adults only, as opposed to total people or children.

Conclusion: **Controversial speech should be allowed, provided it does not incite major violence.**

> Avoid extreme words in answer choices.

The boundary phrase **provided it does not incite major violence** limits the scope of the conclusion. It restricts the meaning to most types of controversial speech, as opposed to all types of controversial speech. The boundary word **major** limits the exception. Controversial speech should not be allowed when it incites major violence, as opposed to any violence.

Boundary words and phrases are vital because they provide the nuance of the argument. Many Critical Reasoning questions hinge on whether you understand and can apply the boundaries of an argument. Boundary words should always be underlined in your diagrams.

General Strategy: Extreme Words

Another general strategy for all Critical Reasoning questions involves EXTREME words and phrases. Extreme words and phrases do the opposite of boundary words. Using extreme words opens up an argument unreasonably, making the argument very susceptible to attack. For example:

Conclusion: **Sugar is never healthy for anyone trying to lose weight.**

The extreme word **never** unreasonably opens up this argument, putting no limitation on the claim that sugar is unhealthy. A more reasonable conclusion would argue that sugar is **usually unhealthy** or that **excessive sugar is unhealthy**. The extreme word **anyone** further opens up this argument. A more reasonable conclusion might be that this claim applies to *most* people trying to lose weight.

Since extreme words are not parts of good arguments, you should eliminate answer choices that use extreme words and phrases—especially when the question asks you to draw a conclusion or make an inference. Good GMAT conclusions and inferences always use moderate language. They NEVER use extreme words.

General Strategy: "Except" Questions

Sometimes the GMAT will make a question more complex than it needs to be by using the word EXCEPT. The GMAT can manipulate all question types by using this complex EXCEPT formation. In order to combat this complexity, rephrase the EXCEPT statement into a question, inserting the word NOT and eliminating the word EXCEPT.

Each of the following helps to explain event X EXCEPT:

should be rephrased as: Which of the following does NOT help to explain event X?

Each of the following weakens the conclusion EXCEPT:

should be rephrased as: Which of the following does NOT weaken the conclusion?

Each of the following strengthens the conclusion EXCEPT:

should be rephrased as: Which of the following does NOT strengthen the conclusion?

Each of the following makes the argument logically correct EXCEPT:

should be rephrased as: Which of the following does NOT make the argument logically correct?

Rephrase EXCEPT questions to make them easier to understand.

Type 1: Find an Assumption

These questions ask you to identify an assumption upon which the argument is based.

The assumption you select should:
  (1) be closely tied to the conclusion
  (2) support/strengthen the conclusion

When limitations were in effect on nuclear-arms testing, people tended to save more of their money, but when nuclear-arms testing increased, people tended to spend more of their money. The perceived threat of nuclear catastrophe, therefore, decreases the willingness of people to postpone consumption for the sake of saving money.

The argument above assumes that

(A) the perceived threat of nuclear catastrophe has increased over the years
(B) most people supported the development of nuclear arms
(C) people's perception of the threat of nuclear catastrophe depends on the amount of nuclear-arms testing being done
(D) the people who saved the most money when nuclear-arms testing was limited were the ones who supported such limitations
(E) there are more consumer goods available when nuclear-arms testing increases

The Official Guide for GMAT Review (10th edition), #21
GMAT® questions are the property of the Graduate Management
Admission Council® and are reprinted with its permission.

To answer this question, first identify the conclusion:

The perceived threat of nuclear catastrophe decreases the willingness of people to postpone consumption for the sake of saving money.

The assumption must be closely tied to the conclusion. The only answer choice that supports and is closely tied to the conclusion is **(C)**. Note the words **perceived** and **perception**, and the phrase **threat of nuclear catastrophe**.

Note also that this assumption does not assume too much. It merely makes explicit a logical step in the argument: when more nuclear-arms testing is done, people perceive a greater threat of a nuclear catastrophe.

Assumptions are never stated in the argument.

Categories of Assumption

The correct answer to "Find an Assumption" questions almost always falls into one of the following four categories.

1. Assumptions can serve to fill in a logic gap.

Most assumptions simply fill in gaps in the logic or sequence of an argument. They provide additional premises that are needed to draw the conclusion, given the premises in the argument.

> **Amy is less than 5'6" tall. Therefore, she cannot have a successful career as a fashion model.**

In order to make the logical leap from the premise in the first sentence of this argument to the conclusion in the second sentence, we must insert an additional premise. This unstated premise is an assumption.

The correct answer choice might be: **Successful fashion models must be 5'6" or taller.**

2. Assumptions can establish the feasibility of the premises of the argument.

These statements simply say that the premises in the argument can actually be true.

> **Uncle Gabe's get-rich-quick scheme is simple: he will use a metal detector to find hidden treasures in the sand. Then he will sell the treasures to a local pawn broker.**

This argument *assumes* that a metal detector actually can find treasures hidden in the sand. If this is not true, the premise that Gabe will find them with a metal detector is not feasible.

The correct answer choice might be: **Uncle Gabe's metal detector is capable of detecting treasures hidden beneath the sand.**

Don't look for the perfect answer. Instead, focus on eliminating incorrect answers until you have only one choice left.

3. Assumptions can eliminate alternate paths to the same end.
Many GMAT arguments contain linear logic paths: A, B, and C are true, therefore X is true. However, in simple linear paths, the speaker often ignores the possibility of a different path to the same end.

> **Girl Power magazine published an article proclaiming that one can lose up to 20 pounds a month by eating only soup. Kelly concludes that the best way for her to lose 40 pounds is to eat only soup for 2 months.**

When provided with a cause and effect argument, look for an assumption that eliminates alternate models of causation.

This conclusion ignores the many other (probably healthier) ways Kelly could lose 40 pounds. In other words, it *assumes* that there is no better way for her to lose weight than to eat soup.

The correct answer choice might be: **Kelly is unable to lose weight in another way.**

4. Assumptions can eliminate alternate models of causation.
Many GMAT arguments are simply statements of cause and effect. For example:

> **Researchers in the field have noticed that older antelope are more cautious. Therefore, they have concluded that the quality of caution increases with age in antelope.**

This argument outlines a cause and effect relationship: **age** causes **increased caution**. However, the argument ignores the fact that antelope who are cautious may have a better chance of avoiding an attack by predators and may therefore live longer. In order for the conclusion to be valid, the researchers are *assuming* that this alternate model of causation is, in fact, untrue.

The correct answer choice might be: **Increased caution does not enable antelope to live longer.**

Critical Reasoning

Now that you have completed your study of FIND AN ASSUMPTION questions, it is time to test your skills on passages that have actually appeared on real GMAT exams over the past several years.

The problem set that follows is composed of Critical Reasoning passages from two books published by GMAC (Graduate Management Admission Council):

The Official Guide for GMAT Review, 11th Edition (pages 32-38 & 468-504)
The Official Guide for GMAT Verbal Review (pages 116-142)

Continue to diagram each argument, but this time, you should answer each question. Also, try to identify which type of assumption is represented by the correct answer.

Note: Problem numbers preceded by "D" refer to questions in the Diagnostic Test chapter of *The Official Guide for GMAT Review, 11th Edition* (pages 32-38).

Find an Assumption

    11th Edition: D28, 2, 14, 25, 32, 47, 50, 52, 59, 77, 80, 81, 89, 92, 96, 97, 109, 110
    Verbal Review: 7, 13, 34, 45, 51, 56, 63, 75

Type 2: Draw a Conclusion

These questions ask you to draw a conclusion based on a passage of given premises. GMAT conclusions are arguable statements that are supported by the premises of the argument. If you are asked to draw a conclusion, you must be able to support it with only the premises given; the conclusion should not require you to make any additional assumptions at all.

The conclusion you select should:
     (1) never go far beyond the premises AND
     (2) not contain extreme words or phrases, such as ALWAYS, NEVER, or ALL.

The cost of producing radios in Country Q is ten percent less than the cost of producing radios in Country Y. Even after transportation fees and tariff charges are added, it is still cheaper for a company to import radios from Country Q to Country Y than to produce radios in Country Y.

> Be careful not to conclude too much!

The statements above, if true, best support which of the following assertions?

(A) Labor costs in Country Q are ten percent below those in Country Y.
(B) Importing radios from Country Q to Country Y will eliminate ten percent of the manufacturing jobs in Country Y.
(C) The tariff on a radio imported from Country Q to Country Y is less than ten percent of the cost of manufacturing the radio in Country Y.
(D) The fee for transporting a radio from Country Q to Country Y is more than ten percent of the cost of manufacturing the radio in Country Q.
(E) It takes ten percent less time to manufacture a radio in Country Q than it does in Country X.

The Official Guide for GMAT Review (11th edition), #104
GMAT® questions are the property of the Graduate Management
Admission Council® and are reprinted with its permission.

The premises in this argument are:
    1. Country Q production cost is 10% LESS than Country Y production cost.
    2. Even with transportation and tariff fees, it is still cheaper to produce radios in Country Q and then import them into Country Y.

Therefore, you are looking for a conclusion that follows naturally from this information. Eliminate **(A)**, since the argument describes production costs in general, not specifically those associated with labor. Eliminate **(B)**, since the argument does not discuss jobs at all. Eliminate **(D)**, since we have no evidence to support this relationship. Eliminate **(E)**, since the passage does not discuss production time at all. We are left with **(C)**.

Manhattan **GMAT** *Prep*
the new standard

Alternately, it is often helpful to use real numbers to make sense of arguments that contain statistics. For example, let's say that it costs $100 to produce a radio in Country Y. Therefore, it costs $90 to produce a radio in Country Q. If, after tariffs and transportation costs, it *still* costs less than $100 to produce a radio in Country Q, then tariff and transportation costs must be *less than $10* ($100 − $90). Since 10 is 10% of 100, the tariff on a radio is less than 10% of the cost of manufacturing the radio in Country Y.

	Y	**Q**
Production	$100	$90
Tax & Tariff	-	t
TOTAL COST	$100	$90 + t$

$$\$100 > \$90 + t$$
$$10 > t$$

Use real numbers to make sense of statistics. Always pick 100 when dealing with percents.

Note that **(C)** simply summarizes the statistical data you have been given. This is not uncommon on the GMAT. GMAT conclusions NEVER go far beyond the premises. In fact, they often don't go beyond the premises at all. They simply summarize or restate the information supplied in the premises.

Critical Reasoning

Now that you have completed your study of DRAW A CONCLUSION questions, it is time to test your skills on passages that have actually appeared on real GMAT exams over the past several years.

The problem set that follows is composed of Critical Reasoning passages from two books published by GMAC (Graduate Management Admission Council):

The Official Guide for GMAT Review, 11th Edition (pages 32-38 & 468-504)
The Official Guide for GMAT Verbal Review (pages 116-142)

Diagram each argument and answer the question by drawing a conclusion that is supported by the premises in your diagram.

Note: Problem numbers preceded by "D" refer to questions in the Diagnostic Test chapter of *The Official Guide for GMAT Review, 11th Edition* (pages 32-38).

Draw a Conclusion

11th Edition: D24, D31, 6, 19, 31, 35, 46, 51, 56, 57, 60, 66, 71, 75, 76, 95, 101, 104
Verbal Review: 20, 44, 52, 57, 59, 64, 74, 77

Type 3: Strengthen the Conclusion: S-W-Slash Chart

These questions ask you to provide additional support for a given conclusion.

A premise that strengthens the conclusion should:
(1) fix a potential weakness of the conclusion OR
(2) introduce additional supporting evidence.

> **Toughened hiring standards have not been the primary cause of the present staffing shortage in public schools. The shortage of teachers is primarily caused by the fact that in recent years teachers have not experienced any improvements in working conditions and their salaries have not kept pace with salaries in other professions.**
>
> **Which of the following, if true, would most support the claims above?**
>
> **(A) Many teachers already in the profession would not have been hired under the new hiring standards.**
> **(B) Today more teachers are entering the profession with a higher educational level than in the past.**
> **(C) Some teachers have cited higher standards for hiring as a reason for the current staffing shortage.**
> **(D) Many teachers have cited low pay and lack of professional freedom as reasons for their leaving the profession.**
> **(E) Many prospective teaches have cited the new hiring standards as a reason for not entering the profession.**

The Official Guide for GMAT Verbal Review, #31
GMAT® *questions are the property of the Graduate Management Admission Council® and are reprinted with its permission.*

In this argument, the conclusion is that **the staffing shortage in public schools is due to poor working conditions and low salaries, not to the new hiring standards.**

$$\begin{array}{c|c} W & A \\ S & B \\ - & C \\ S & D \\ W & E \end{array}$$

Evaluate each of the answer choices, using an S-W-Slash chart to identify whether each *strengthens* the conclusion (S), *weakens* the conclusion (W), or is *irrelevant* to the conclusion (−). **(A)** weakens the conclusion; it actually supports what the argument is trying to refute. **(B)** possibly strengthens the conclusion; people with higher education levels might be more likely to demand higher salaries and better working conditions. **(C)** is irrelevant to the conclusion; teachers' speculation about the reason for the staffing shortage does not provide evidence either way. **(D)** strengthens the conclusion; teachers who leave the profession have explicitly said that they are leaving because of low pay and lack of professional freedom (poor working conditions). **(E)** weakens the conclusion, indicating that the new hiring standards, and not low salaries and poor working conditions, represent the reason for the staffing shortage.

Manhattan **GMAT** *Prep*
the new standard

Only **(B)** and **(D)** strengthen the conclusion. **(B)** is a possible explanation for why teachers are demanding better working conditions and higher salaries, but it requires the assumption that people with a higher education level are more likely to demand better working conditions and higher salaries. **(D)** assumes nothing; it merely tells you that teachers *who have left the profession* (indicated by the word **their** in the answer choice) have given low pay and poor working conditions as explanations for leaving. Since **(D)** requires no assumptions or logical leaps on your part, it is the better answer.

The S-W-Slash chart is an essential tool for eliminating incorrect answer choices. It usually helps you narrow the possible answers down to two choices and prevents you from getting distracted by complicated wording in the question.

Before you analyze each answer choice, be sure to identify the conclusion of the argument.

Type 4: Weaken the Conclusion: S-W-Slash Chart

These questions ask you to weaken the given conclusion.

A premise that weakens the conclusion should:
  (1) expose a faulty assumption OR
  (2) introduce a piece of detracting evidence.

The ice on the front windshield of the car had formed when moisture condensed during the night. The ice melted quickly after the car was warmed up the next morning because the defrosting vent, which blows only on the front windshield, was turned on full force.

Which of the following, if true, most seriously jeopardizes the validity of the explanation for the speed with which the ice melted?

(A) The side windows had no ice condensation on them.
(B) Even though no attempt was made to defrost the back window, the ice there melted at the same rate as did the ice on the front windshield.
(C) The speed at which ice on a window melts increases as the temperature of the air blown on the windshield increases.
(D) The warm air from the defrosting vent for the front windshield cools rapidly as it dissipates throughout the rest of the car.
(E) The defrosting vent operates efficiently even when the heater, which blows warm air toward the feet or faces of the driver and passengers, is on.

The Official Guide for GMAT Review (10th edition), #7
GMAT® questions are the property of the Graduate Management Admission Council® and are reprinted with its permission.

In this argument, the conclusion is that **the defrosting vent caused the ice on the front windshield to melt quickly.**

Evaluate each of the answer choices using an S-W-Slash chart. **(C)** actually supports the conclusion. **(A)**, **(D)**, and **(E)** neither support nor weaken the conclusion; they simply present irrelevant information. Only **(B)** weakens the conclusion by exposing a faulty assumption. The argument assumes that the ice melted quickly because of the defrosting vent; however, the ice on the back windshield, where there was no defrosting vent, melted just as quickly.

Critical Reasoning

Now that you have completed your study of STRENGTHEN and WEAKEN questions, it is time to test your skills on passages that have actually appeared on real GMAT exams over the past several years.

The problem set that follows is composed of Critical Reasoning passages from two books published by GMAC (Graduate Management Admission Council):

The Official Guide for GMAT Review, 11th Edition (pages 32-38 & 468-504)
The Official Guide for GMAT Verbal Review (pages 116-142)

Diagram each argument and answer the question by using an S-W-Slash Chart. Remember, begin by identifying whether each answer choice *strengthens the conclusion, weakens the conclusion,* or *neither strengthens nor weakens the conclusion.* Then, eliminate answer choices based on your chart.

Note: Problem numbers preceded by "D" refer to questions in the Diagnostic Test chapter of *The Official Guide for GMAT Review, 11th Edition* (pages 32-38).

Strengthen the Conclusion

11th Edition: D25, D27, D32, 7, 9, 13, 16, 26, 28, 30, 36, 37, 41, 43, 53, 54, 63, 67, 69, 73, 103, 112, 114, 117, 123

Verbal Review: 1, 3, 16, 22, 25, 31, 33, 35, 36, 53, 55, 67, 68, 69, 70, 71, 80

Weaken the Conclusion

11th Edition: D18, D20, D23, D26, D30, D34, 1, 3, 10, 12, 15, 17, 18, 20, 23, 27, 33, 38, 39, 40, 42, 44, 48, 55, 61, 62, 64, 65, 68, 72, 78, 79, 83, 84, 85, 86, 88, 91, 93, 98, 100, 102, 105, 107, 111, 113, 115, 116, 118, 120, 121, 122, 124

Verbal Review: 4, 6, 11, 15, 17, 18, 19, 21, 24, 26, 27, 28, 29, 32, 37, 39, 40, 46, 47, 48, 49, 50, 54, 58, 60, 62, 76, 79, 81

Type 5: Analyze the Argument Structure

These questions hinge on your ability to understand how GMAT arguments are structured. Typically these questions present pieces of the argument in boldfaced type and ask you to analyze the role that these pieces play in the structure of the argument. Recently, this type of question has become significantly more common.

When answering questions of this type, diagram the argument, so that you can identify the conclusion before you evaluate the boldfaced portions. Then, decide how the bold-faced sections of the argument relate to the conclusion and to each other, evaluating one portion at a time.

This problem type has recently become much more common.

Consumer advocate: It is generally true, at least in this state, that lawyers who advertise a specific service charge less for that service than lawyers who do not advertise. It is also true that **each time restrictions on the advertising of legal services have been eliminated, the number of lawyers advertising their services has increased and legal costs to consumers have declined in consequence**. However, eliminating the state requirement that legal advertisements must specify fees for specific services would almost certainly increase rather than further reduce consumers' legal costs. Lawyers would no longer have an incentive to lower their fees when they begin advertising and **if no longer required to specify fee arrangements, many lawyers who now advertise would increase their fees**.

In the consumer advocate's argument, the two portions in *boldface* play which of the following roles?

(A) The first is a generalization that the consumer advocate accepts as true; the second is presented as a consequence that follows from the truth of that generalization.

(B) The first is a pattern of cause and effect that the consumer advocate argues will be repeated in the case at issue; the second acknowledges a circumstance in which that pattern would not hold.

(C) The first is a pattern of cause and effect that the consumer advocate predicts will not hold in the case at issue; the second offers a consideration in support of that prediction.

(D) The first is evidence that the consumer advocate offers in support of a certain prediction; the second is that prediction.

(E) The first acknowledges a consideration that weighs against the main position that the consumer advocate defends; the second is that position.

The Official Guide for GMAT Verbal Review, #82

GMAT® questions are the property of the Graduate Management Admission Council® and are reprinted with its permission.

In this argument, the conclusion is that **eliminating the requirement that legal advertisements must specify fees would increase consumer's legal costs.** This is the point the consumer advocate is trying to argue, or defend. It is the final logical step in the consumer advocate's reasoning.

Evaluate the portions of the argument in boldface as to how they relate to this conclusion. First,

...each time restrictions on the advertising of legal services have been eliminated, the number of lawyers advertising their services has increased and legal costs to consumers have declined in consequence.

Is this: (A) a generalization that the consumer advocate accepts as true,

(B) a pattern of cause and effect that will be repeated,

(C) a pattern of cause and effect that will NOT hold true,

(D) evidence in support of the increase in legal costs, OR

(E) a consideration that weighs against the increase in legal costs?

You can eliminate **(B)** and **(D)**. The consumer advocate argues that this pattern will NOT hold true in this case and notes that the pattern does not support the predicted increase in legal costs.

Then, consider the second boldfaced portion. Do not bother to evaluate the answer choices you have already eliminated.

...if no longer required to specify fee arrangements, many lawyers who now advertise would increase their fees.

Is this: (A) a consequence of the generalization described in the first boldfaced portion,

(C) a consideration that supports the predicted increase in legal costs, OR

(E) the conclusion itself?

Clearly, **(E)** is incorrect. This is not the ultimate conclusion of the passage. In regards to choice **(A)**, the second boldfaced portion actually is not a consequence of the generalization described in the first boldfaced portion; it contradicts this generalization. Therefore, the correct answer is **(C)**.

For "Analyze the Argument Structure" questions, it is critical that you begin by diagramming the argument and identifying the conclusion. Then, analyze how each boldfaced portion of the passage relates to the conclusion, one portion at a time. Remember that sometimes one of the boldfaced portions will be the conclusion itself.

Note that not all "Analyze the Argument Structure" questions involve comparing boldfaced portions. Sometimes, you are asked how an author develops an argument or what roles different individuals play in a given argument. In each instance, diagramming (with a particular focus on locating the conclusion) is the key to understanding how an argument is structured.

Critical Reasoning

Now that you have completed your study of ANALYZE THE ARGUMENT STRUCTURE questions, it is time to test your skills on passages that have actually appeared on real GMAT exams over the past several years.

The problem set that follows is composed of Critical Reasoning passages from two books published by GMAC (Graduate Management Admission Council):

The Official Guide for GMAT Review, 11th Edition (pages 468-504)
The Official Guide for GMAT Verbal Review (pages 116-142)

Diagram each argument and answer the question by analyzing the structure of the passage.

Analyze the Argument Structure
 11th Edition: 87, 90, 94
 Verbal Review: 82

Minor Question Types

Aside from the five major question types, there are a variety of minor question types that the GMAT uses for Critical Reasoning passages. These are outlined below:

Explain an event or discrepancy:
The question generally poses two seemingly contradictory premises and asks you to find the answer choice that best reconciles them.

> Example: **Which of the following statements, if true, would best explain the sudden drop in temperature?**

Make an inference about a passage of premises:
The question asks you to make an informed deduction about a passage of premises. A GMAT inference is very moderate and rarely goes far beyond the premises. You should generally infer so little that the inference seems obvious. This is very similar to the strategy for answering Draw a Conclusion questions.

> Example: **Which of the following can be correctly inferred from the statements above?**

Evaluate the conclusion:
The question asks you to evaluate the validity of a given conclusion or to suggest a way in which one could efficiently evaluate a given conclusion. You should generally consider assumptions upon which the argument is based in choosing your answer.

> Example: **Which of the following is most likely to yield information that would help to evaluate the effectiveness of the new method?**

Resolve a problem:
The question asks you to solve a problem posed by a passage of premises. You should use the specific details in the premises as the basis of your solution.

> Example: **Which of the following would best counteract the drug's effects?**

Provide an example:
The question asks you to select a situation that best exemplifies the main point (the conclusion) of a given argument.

> Example: **Which of the following illustrates the process described above?**

Restate the conclusion:
The question asks you to find the main point–the conclusion–of the passage. Use your diagram to locate the conclusion and choose the answer choice that restates it.

> Example: **Which of the following statements best summarizes the main point of the argument above?**

Mimic the argument:
The question asks you to analyze the logical flow of an argument and then choose the answer choice that most closely mimics this line of reasoning.

> Example: **Which of the following arguments is most similar to the line of reasoning in the argument above?**

Identifying the question type will help you apply an effective strategy.

*Manhattan*GMAT*Prep
the new standard

Critical Reasoning

Now that you have completed your study of MINOR QUESTION TYPES, it is time to test your skills on passages that have actually appeared on real GMAT exams over the past several years.

The problem set that follows is composed of Critical Reasoning passages from two books published by GMAC (Graduate Management Admission Council):

The Official Guide for GMAT Review, 11th Edition (pages 32-38 & 468-504)
The Official Guide for GMAT Verbal Review (pages 116-142)

Diagram each argument and answer each question.

Note: Problem numbers preceded by "D" refer to questions in the Diagnostic Test chapter of *The Official Guide for GMAT Review, 11th Edition* (pages 32-38).

Explain an Event or Discrepancy
>   *11th Edition:* D19, D33, 4, 11, 22, 45, 49, 74, 82, 99, 119
>   *Verbal Review:* 9, 23, 61, 66, 72, 73

Make an Inference about Premises
>   *11th Edition:* 21, 34, 70
>   *Verbal Review:* 2, 12, 14, 43

Evaluate the Conclusion
>   *11th Edition:* D21, D22, D29, 5, 24, 106, 108
>   *Verbal Review:* 41, 65, 78

Resolve a Problem
>   *11th Edition:* 8, 58
>   *Verbal Review:* 30, 10

Provide an Example
>   *Verbal Review:* 5, 38

Restate the Conclusion
>   *11th Edition:* 29
>   *Verbal Review:* 42

Mimic the Argument
>   *Verbal Review:* 8

Reading Comprehension

Chapter 4

of

CRITICAL REASONING & READING COMPREHENSION

LONG vs. SHORT

In This Chapter . . .

LONG VS. SHORT

GMAT Reading Comprehension passages come in two basic forms: LONG and SHORT. Differentiating your reading strategy based on these two forms is the primary key to Reading Comprehension success.

Each GMAT reading passage is accompanied by line numbers, making it easy to identify a passage as either LONG or SHORT. On the real GMAT CAT exam, a long passage is anything over 50 lines, and a short passage is anything under 50 lines. (Note that this number is strictly for the real computer-based test; in *The Official Guide for GMAT Review, 11th Edition* and *The Official Guide for GMAT Verbal Review*, the long-short line cutoff is 35. Other practice guides and simulated software programs may contain different cutoff numbers.)

You can expect to see 4 Reading Comprehension passages on the GMAT. Each passage will typically be accompanied by about 3 to 5 questions, for a total of about 14 Reading Comprehension questions. Due to the computerized format of the exam, the questions are presented ONE AT A TIME on the right side of the computer screen, while the complete reading passage remains on the left side of the screen throughout. Since questions are presented one at a time, and you cannot return to questions after skipping them, it is unfortunately not possible to read all the questions first before reading the passage. You must review the passage first.

Thus, the key to your success lies in HOW you read the passage the first time through, before knowing all of the questions.

On the CAT, you will only be able to see the first question before you read the passage.

Long Passages: An Overview

LONG passages are those that have more than 50 lines of text on the computer screen (easily seen by the accompanying line numbers). These passages average between 70 and 90 lines of text and are often accompanied by 4-5 questions, although this varies.

Note that although questions appear one at a time, the GMAT does inform you of how many questions will accompany a given passage. The top of each passage gives you this information (for example, the top of a given passage may read **questions 6 to 10**, so you know there are 5 questions that will accompany this passage).

All passages on the GMAT relate to one of three topic areas: Social Science, Science, or Business. Although these topics can be interesting, the GMAT makes them as boring and tedious as possible by using dry, clinical language, replete with long, detail-laden sentences.

The basic problem with a LONG PASSAGE is that there is too much information to absorb in one sustained reading. Additionally, there is not enough time to outline the entire passage, with all its details and nuances. Moreover, without knowing what the questions are, it is impossible to know what to focus on in an initial reading. The solution is to create a SKELETAL SKETCH of the passage during your first reading. A Skeletal Sketch serves several purposes:

(1)   It fosters retention of the text by using writing to promote active reading.
(2)   It provides a general sketch of the text without getting bogged down in details.
(3)   It promotes a faster first reading of long, complex passages, so that more time can be spent on answering the questions.

Do not try to read an entire long passage before seeing the questions. Instead, skim the passage and create a Skeletal Sketch.

The Skeletal Sketch

The creation of a Skeletal Sketch has several key elements:

(1)   Just as the top of a skeleton (the skull) is its most defined feature, so too the first paragraph of every long passage gives shape to the text. As such, your Skeletal Sketch requires a defined "skull." In it, you should carefully outline the first paragraph, paying attention to all its major points.

(2)   The limbs of your Skeletal Sketch are simply the topic sentences of the remaining paragraphs. Each paragraph has one topic sentence that gives the main point of the paragraph. Generally, the topic sentence is the first or second sentence, although it can also be a combination of the two. The topic sentences should be organized as a bulleted list under the skeletal "skull."

(3)   After sketching the topic sentence of a given paragraph, SKIM the rest, recording only key words. Key words include names, places, and terms. **You should not read these sections.** In fact, reading them is often a bad idea, since you can get lost in the details, which takes you away from the purpose of your sketch: to understand the overall structure of the passage. This is where you can save much of your time.

How is the Skeletal Sketch used in answering the questions?

The Skeletal Sketch provides ready-made answers to all GENERAL question types. These are questions that pertain to the main idea of the passage, the purpose of the passage, and the structure or form of the passage, as well as questions that relate to the author's style and objectives. These general questions can be answered directly by reviewing your Skeletal Sketch.

The Skeletal Sketch also provides a search tool for answering all SPECIFIC question types. These are detail-oriented questions, which can only be answered by returning to the text of the passage. Using the limbs of your skeletal sketch, you can determine which paragraph you need to read in order to find a particular detail.

Using your sketch to answer questions will be discussed in the next section on Question Types.

A skeletal sketch allows you to read each section of the passage only when you are answering a question that pertains to it.

Sketching Real Examples

Sketching is a powerful strategy that is best learned by repeated practice with REAL GMAT reading passages. The following examples provide model Skeletal Sketches for LONG passages taken from *The Official Guide for GMAT Review, 10th edition* and *The Official Guide for GMAT Verbal Review*.

PASSAGE 1

Read the first paragraph and take notes. Then jot down the topic sentences of the subsequent paragraphs, along with key words.

Two divergent definitions have dominated sociologists' discussions of the nature of ethnicity. The first emphasizes the primordial and unchanging character of ethnicity. In this view, people have an essential need for belonging that is satisfied by membership in groups based on shared ancestry and culture. A different conception of ethnicity de-emphasizes the cultural component and defines ethnic groups as interest groups. In this view, ethnicity serves as a way of mobilizing a certain population behind issues relating to its economic position. While both of these definitions are useful, neither fully captures the dynamic and changing aspects of ethnicity in the United States. Rather, ethnicity is more satisfactorily conceived of as a process in which preexisting communal bonds and common cultural attributes are adapted for instrumental purposes according to changing real-life situations.

One example of this process is the rise of participation by Native American people in the broader United States political system since the Civil Rights movement of the 1960's. Besides leading Native Americans to participate more actively in politics (the number of Native American legislative officeholders more than doubled), this movement also evoked increased interest in tribal history and traditional culture. Cultural and instrumental components of ethnicity are not mutually exclusive, but rather reinforce one another.

The Civil Rights movement also brought changes in the uses to which ethnicity was put by Mexican American people. In the 1960's, Mexican Americans formed community-based political groups that emphasized ancestral heritage as a way of mobilizing constituents. Such emerging issues as immigration and voting rights gave Mexican American advocacy groups the means by which to promote ethnic solidarity. Like European ethnic groups in the nineteenth-century United States, late-twentieth-century Mexican American leaders combined ethnic with contemporary civic symbols. In 1968 Henry Cisneros, later mayor of San Antonio, Texas, cited Mexican leader Benito Juarez as a model for Mexican Americans in their fight for contemporary civil rights. And every year, Mexican Americans celebrate Cinco de Mayo as fervently as many Irish American people embrace St. Patrick's Day (both are major holidays in the countries of origin), with both holidays having been reinvented in the context of the United States and linked to ideals, symbols, and heroes of the United States.

The following is a Skeletal Sketch of the preceding passage:

*Two views of ethnicity:
1. Primordial and unchanging view: people have essential need for belonging, satisfied by group based on shared ancestry/culture
2. Interest groups view: de-emphasizes cultural component, mobilizes group behind economic issues

*Both views useful but neither captures ethnicity in US

*Better: Ethnicity is PROCESS in which preexisting bonds + culture are adapted for use in changing real-life situations

→ Example: Rise of participation by Native Americans in US politics since Civil Rights movement in 1960's
POLITICS, TRIBAL HISTORY, REINFORCE

→ Civil Rights movement caused change in Mexican-American use of ethnicity
IMMIGRATION, VOTING RIGHTS, EUROPEANS, CISNEROS, JUAREZ, CINCO DE MAYO, IRISH-AMERICANS, ST. PATRICK'S DAY

Notice that the "skull" of the sketch—the boxed section—includes the most detail, as it carefully outlines the major points of the first paragraph. The skull of this passage, as is often the case, closely resembles a GMAT argument (with premises and a conclusion).

The limbs of the sketch—one for the second paragraph and one for the third paragraph—are each very concise, consisting only of a topic sentence and key words.

You should have the most detail in the skull of your sketch.

PASSAGE 2

Remember, do not read any entire paragraphs other than the first.

Caffeine, the stimulant in coffee, has been called "the most widely used psychoactive substance on Earth." Snyder, Daly, and Bruns have recently proposed that caffeine affects behavior by countering the activity in the human brain of a naturally occurring chemical called adenosine. Adenosine normally depresses neuron firing in many areas of the brain. It apparently does this by inhibiting the release of neurotransmitters, chemicals that carry nerve impulses from one neuron to the next. Like many other agents that affect neuron firing, adenosine must first bind to specific receptors on neuronal membranes. There are at least two classes of these receptors, which have been designated A_1 and A_2. Snyder et al propose that caffeine, which is structurally similar to adenosine, is able to bind to both types of receptors, which prevents adenosine from attaching there and allows the neurons to fire more readily than they otherwise would.

For many years, caffeine's effects have been attributed to its inhibition of the production of phosphodiesterase, an enzyme that breaks down the chemical called cyclic AMP. A number of neurotransmitters exert their effects by first increasing cyclic AMP concentrations in target neurons. Therefore, prolonged periods at the elevated concentrations, as might be brought about by a phosphodiesterase inhibitor, could lead to a greater amount of neuron firing and, consequently, to behavioral stimulation. But Snyder et al point out that the caffeine concentrations needed to inhibit the production of phosphodiesterase in the brain are much higher than those that produce stimulation. Moreover, other compounds that block phophodiesterase's activity are not stimulants.

To buttress their case that caffeine acts instead by preventing adenosine binding, Snyder et al compared the stimulatory effects of a series of caffeine derivatives with their ability to dislodge adenosine from its receptors in the brains of mice. "In general," they reported, "the ability of the compounds to compete at the receptors correlates with their ability to stimulate locomotion in the mouse; i.e., the higher their capacity to bind at the receptors, the higher their ability to stimulate locomotion." Theophylline, a close structural relative of caffeine and the major stimulant in tea, was one of the most effective compounds in both regards.

There were some apparent exceptions to the general correlation observed between adenosine-receptor binding and stimulation. One of these was a compound called 3-isobutyl-1-methylxanthine (IBMX), which bound very well but actually depressed mouse locomotion. Snyder et al suggest that this is not a major stumbling block to their hypothesis. The problem is that the compound has mixed effects in the brain, a not unusual occurrence with psychoactive drugs. Even caffeine, which is generally known only for its stimulatory effects, displays this property, depressing mouse locomotion at very low concentrations and stimulating it at higher ones.

The Official Guide for GMAT Verbal Review, page 44

The following is a Skeletal Sketch for the preceding passage:

---

*S, D, B propose: Caffeine counters adenosine in human brain

*Adenosine normally slows neuron firing by slowing release of neuro-transmitters

*Adenosine has to bind to receptors (A_1 and A_2) on neurons

*Caffeine—structurally similar to adenosine—binds to receptors instead, allowing neurons to fire

---

The topic sentence of each paragraph is usually the first sentence.

→ Previously: Caffeine slows production of phosphodiesterase, enzyme that breaks down AMP
NEUROTRANSMITTERS, AMP CONCENTRATION, BLOCK PHOSPHO ACTIVITY

→ To bolster case, S, D, B tested caffeine derivatives to see if their ability to dislodge adenosine from its receptors stimulated mice
STIMULATE LOCOMOTION, THEOPHYLLINE, TEA

→ Exceptions to correlation between adenosine-receptor binding + stimulation
IBMX, DEPRESSED LOCOMOTION, MIXED EFFECTS, PSYCHO-ACTIVE DRUGS

The "skull" of this sketch carefully reconstructs the scientists' hypothesis, which is explained in the first paragraph. The limbs are the summarized topic sentences and key words from each of the subsequent three paragraphs. Note that all the topic sentences are, as is usually the case, the first sentence of each paragraph.

Short Passages: An Overview

SHORT passages are those that have less than 50 lines of text on the computer screen (easily seen by the accompanying line numbers). These passages average between 30 and 45 lines of text and are generally accompanied by around 3 questions, although this varies.

SHORT passages are similar to LONG passages in several ways. First, all SHORT passages cover the same three topic areas—Social Science, Science, and Business. Second, SHORT passages still contain those tedious, dry, detail-laden GMAT sentences. Finally, despite their relative brevity, SHORT passages still contain too much information to absorb in one sustained reading.

> For a short passage, you should read the entire passage and take notes.

However, in contrast to LONG passages, there is sufficient time to outline SHORT passages in their entirety. Instead of a Skeletal Sketch, then, you should employ a DETAIL MAP when you see a SHORT reading passage on the GMAT.

A DETAIL MAP serves several purposes:

(1)   It fosters retention of the text by using writing to promote active reading.
(2)   It provides the general structure of the text.
(3)   It outlines key details of the text, promoting a thorough first reading.

The Detail Map

The creation of a Detail Map has several key elements:

(1)   Read the topic sentence of the first paragraph completely. Then summarize it concisely and underline your summary sentence.

(2)   Continue reading the paragraph, one sentence at a time. These sentences are detail sentences which develop the major point given in the topic sentence. Summarize each detail sentence concisely, listing each one underneath the topic sentence.

(3)   Repeat this process for any subsequent paragraphs.

The Detail Map is designed to be thorough enough to provide answers to almost all Reading Comprehension question types. Thus, you will not need to look back in the passage to find answers very frequently. In some cases, however, you will need to return to the passage. Your detail sentences will then serve as pinpoint search tools for locating the exact place in the passage that will provide the answer to the question given.

Using your Detail Map to answer questions will be discussed further in the later section on Question Types.

Detail Maps for Real Examples

Using Detail Maps is best learned by repeated practice with REAL GMAT reading passages. The following examples provide model Detail Maps for SHORT passages taken from *The Official Guide for GMAT Review (11th Edition)*.

PASSAGE 3

Australian researchers have discovered electroreceptors (sensory organs designed to respond to electrical fields) clustered at the tip of the spiny anteater's snout. The researchers made this discovery by exposing small areas of the snout to extremely weak electrical fields and recording the transmission of resulting nervous activity to the brain. While it is true that tactile receptors, another kind of sensory organ on the anteater's snout, can also respond to electrical stimuli, such receptors do so only in response to electrical field strengths about 1,000 times greater than those known to excite electroreceptors.

Having discovered the electroreceptors, researchers are now investigating how anteaters utilize such a sophisticated sensory system. In one behavioral experiment, researchers successfully trained an anteater to distinguish between two troughs of water, one with a weak electrical field and the other with none. Such evidence is consistent with researchers' hypothesis that anteaters use electroreceptors to detect electrical signals given off by prey; however, researchers as yet have been unable to detect electrical signals emanating from termite mounds, where the favorite food of anteaters live. Still, researchers have observed anteaters breaking into a nest of ants at an oblique angle and quickly locating nesting chambers. This ability to quickly locate unseen prey suggests, according to the researchers, that the anteaters were using their electroreceptors to locate the nesting chambers.

> Your detail map should include topic sentences and supporting details for each paragraph in the passage.

The Official Guide for GMAT Review (11th edition), page 370
GMAT® questions are the property of the Graduate Management Admission Council® and are reprinted with its permission.

The following is a Detail Map of the preceding SHORT passage:

Researchers: electroreceptors at tip of anteater's snout
   → Discovery: Exposed small parts of snout to weak electric fields + recorded brain activity
   → Tactile receptors on snout only respond to stronger fields

Investigation: How anteaters utilize electroreceptors
   → Experiment: trained to distinguish water troughs by electric field
   → Hypothesis: use receptors to detect signals given off by prey
   → No signals detected yet from termites, though anteaters locate them very quickly

The two underlined summaries concisely capture the topic sentence of each paragraph. They are each followed by a list that summarizes the key details of each paragraph.

*Manhattan*GMAT®Prep
the new standard

PASSAGE 4

Traditionally, the first firm to commercialize a new technology has benefited from the unique opportunity to shape product definitions, forcing followers to adapt to a standard or invest in an unproven alternative. Today, however, the largest payoffs may go to companies that lead in developing integrated approaches for successful mass production and distribution.

Producers of the Beta format for videocassette recorders (VCR's), for example, were first to develop the VCR commercially in 1974, but producers of the rival VHS (Video Home System) format proved to be more successful at forming strategic alliances with other producers and distributors to manufacture and market their VCR format. Seeking to maintain exclusive control over VCR distribution, Beta producers were reluctant to form such alliances and eventually lost ground to VHS in the competition for the global VCR market.

Despite Beta's substantial technological head start and the fact that VHS was neither technically better nor cheaper than Beta, developers of VHS quickly turned a slight early lead in sales into a dominant position. Strategic alignments with producers of prerecorded tapes reinforced the VHS advantage. The perception among consumers that prerecorded tapes were more available in VHS format further expanded VHS's share of the market. By the end of the 1980's, Beta was no longer in production.

The following is a Detail Map of the preceding SHORT passage:

Past: First firm to commercialize product benefited by shaping product definition

Today: Advantage to companies leading in integrated strategy for mass production + distribution

1975: Beta developed first VCR
→ Rival VHS more successful at strategic alliances w/producers + distributors
→ Beta lost ground in global VCR market

Despite Beta's head start, VHS turned slight lead into dominant position
→ VHS aligned with producers of prerecorded tapes to reinforce advantage
→ Consumer Perception: VHS tapes more available
→ Late 1980s: Beta is dead

Notice that, in this example, both sentences of the first paragraph combine to form the main topic. Thus, both are underlined.

the new standard

The main idea of a paragraph can be comprised of more than one sentence.

Chapter 5
of
CRITICAL REASONING & READING COMPREHENSION

QUESTION TYPES

In This Chapter . . .

- General Questions: Point System
- Specific Questions
- Strategies for All Reading Comprehension Questions
- The Seven Strategies for Reading Comprehension
- Analyzing Real Comprehension Questions

QUESTION TYPES

GMAT Reading Comprehension questions come in a variety of forms, but they can essentially be placed into 2 major categories:

1. GENERAL questions
2. SPECIFIC questions

General Questions: Point System

General questions deal with the main idea, purpose, organization, and structure of a passage. Typical general questions are phrased as follows:

> **The primary purpose of the passage is**
> **The main topic of the passage is**
> **The author's primary objective in the passage is**
> **Which of the following best describes the organization of the passage?**
> **The passage as a whole can best be characterized as which of the following?**

The correct answer to general questions such as *What is the main idea of this passage?*, should relate to as much of the passage as possible.

> **STRATEGY: If you are stuck between two answer choices, use a point system to assign a value to each one.**

Assign the answer choice 2 points if it relates to the first paragraph. If the answer choice relates to other paragraphs, assign it 1 point for each of these paragraphs. The answer choice with more points is usually the correct one. In the event of a tie, select the answer choice that pertains to the first paragraph over any choices that do not.

Your Skeletal Sketch provides the key to answering general questions. You should be able to answer general questions without having to read the entire passage. In fact, reading the entire passage can actually be distracting. At least one of the incorrect answer choices will usually pertain to a key detail contained in only one of the body paragraphs. If you have not read these isolated details, you will not be tempted to select these incorrect answer choices.

General questions can often be answered without having to read the entire passage.

Specific Questions

Specific questions deal with details, inferences, assumptions, and arguments. Typical specific questions are phrased as follows:

> **According to the passage**
> **It can be inferred from the passage that**
> **All of the following statements are supported by the passage EXCEPT**
> **Which of the following is an assumption underlying the statement that**

Although you can answer general questions without having read the details contained in the passage, you will need to use the details in the passage to answer the specific questions. However, you should use your Skeletal Sketch or Detail Map to identify the paragraph of the passage that contains the details that are relevant to the question.

> **STRATEGY: Identify the words in the question that you are most likely to find in the passage. Then, go back to the passage and find those key words.**

Consider the limbs of the Skeletal Sketch below:

> → In reality, standardized tests have very little predictive validity
> SAT, COLLEGE GRADES, NORM-REFERENCED, MACHINE-SCORING

> → Speeded test implies that being fast and being smart are the same, but this is not the case
> GORDON, WOMEN, LEARNING DISABILITY, SPEED-READING

> → Tests are biased against students for whom English is not first language
> SPANISH, CULTURAL BIAS

If presented with the question:

> **Robinson raises the issue of cultural bias to do which of the following?**

you should use the limbs of your skeletal sketch to decide that the key words in the question — **cultural bias** — will most likely be found in the last paragraph. Sometimes, you will need to find a synonym for the key words in the question. For example, if the question addresses **weapons of mass destruction**, you may need to find a paragraph that addresses **nuclear and chemical weapons**.

Once you identify the relevant paragraph, you should reread it to answer the question.

> **STRATEGY: You should be able to find ONE or TWO sentences in this paragraph to defend the correct answer choice.**

Only a small handful of GMAT questions require more than two sentences to defend the correct answer choice.

Strategies for All Reading Comprehension Questions

There are several question-attack strategies that you should implement for all Reading Comprehension passages. These include:

1) JUSTIFY every word in the answer choice.

In the correct answer choice, every word should be completely true and within the scope of the passage. If you cannot justify *every* word in the answer choice, eliminate it. For example, consider the answer choices below:

> **(A) The colonists resented the king for taxing them without representation.**
> **(B) England's policy of taxation without representation caused resentment among the colonists.**

The difference in these two answer choices lies in the word **king** versus the word **England**. Although this seems like a small difference, it is the key to eliminating one of these answer choices. If the passage does not mention the king when it discusses the colonists' resentment, then the word **king** cannot be justified, and the answer choice should be eliminated.

2) AVOID extreme words.

Just as you learned to stay away from Critical Reasoning answer choices that use extreme words, so too you should avoid Reading Comprehension answer choices that use extreme words. These words — such as **all**, **never**, etc. — unnecessarily broaden the scope of an answer choice. The GMAT always prefers moderate language and ideas.

3) INFER as little as possible.

Many Reading Comprehension questions ask you to infer something from the passage. An inference is an informed deduction based on the information in the passage. Just as with Critical Reasoning inferences, Reading Comprehension inferences rarely go far beyond what is stated in the passage. In general, you should infer so little that the inference seems obvious.

4) PREVIEW the first question.

As you are reading through a passage for the first time and creating either a Skeletal Sketch or a Detail Map, you will not know all the questions which you will have to answer relating to that passage (as the questions appear on the computer screen one at a time). However, you will know the FIRST question, as this appears on the screen initially, together with the passage. It is important to read this question before reading the passage so that you can have one question in the back of your mind while you read and sketch. Often this first question is a GENERAL question (e.g. **What is the purpose of the passage?**), but sometimes it is a SPECIFIC question that focuses on a particular detail or section of the passage. Knowing the question before you read can help you to focus and save time later.

Read the first question before you read the passage.

The Seven Strategies for Reading Comprehension

In summary, there are seven effective strategies you can use to answer Reading Comprehension questions on the GMAT. You may wish to jot these strategies down on your scratch paper before beginning the verbal section on test day. At the very least, you should commit them to memory and use them when you practice answering questions.

For GENERAL questions:

(1)   Use a **POINT SYSTEM** when stuck between two answer choices.

For SPECIFIC questions:

(2)   Match **KEY WORDS** in specific questions to key words (or synonyms) in the passage.

(3)   **DEFEND** your answer choice with 1-2 sentences.

For ALL questions:

(4)   **JUSTIFY** every word in your answer choice.

(5)   Avoid answer choices that contain **EXTREME** words.

(6)   Choose an answer choice that **INFERS** as **LITTLE** as possible.

And don't forget to:

(7)   **PREVIEW** the first question before reading the passage.

Some strategies that apply to Critical Reasoning questions also apply to Reading Comprehension questions.

Analyzing Real Comprehension Questions

Answering Reading Comprehension questions is best learned by repeated practice with REAL GMAT passages and questions. The following examples use passages and questions taken from *The Official Guide for GMAT Review (10th edition)*, *The Official Guide for GMAT Review (11th edition)*, and *The Official Guide for GMAT Verbal Review*. These passages are the same ones used as examples in the previous section covering LONG vs. SHORT passages. Now, we will use the Skeletal Sketches and Detail Maps that we created for each passage in order to answer REAL questions.

Please refer back to the previous section or to *The Official Guide for GMAT Review, 10th edition* (page 388) in order to reread **Passage 1**. Below is the Skeletal Sketch for this passage:

*Two views of ethnicity:
1. Primordial and unchanging view: people have essential need for belonging, satisfied by group based on shared ancestry/culture
2. Interest groups view: de-emphasizes cultural component, mobilizes group behind economic issues

*Both views useful but neither captures ethnicity in US

*Better: Ethnicity is PROCESS in which preexisting bonds + culture are adapted for use in changing real-life situations

→ Example: Rise of participation by Native Americans in US politics since Civil Rights movement in 1960's
POLITICS, TRIBAL HISTORY, REINFORCE

→ Civil Rights movement caused change in Mexican-American use of ethnicity
IMMIGRATION, VOTING RIGHTS, EUROPEANS, CISNEROS, JUAREZ, CINCO DE MAYO, IRISH AMERICANS, ST. PATRICK'S DAY

Remember the 7 Strategies for Reading Comprehension.

QUESTION TYPES STRATEGY

Which of the following best states the main idea of the passage?

(A)   In their definitions of the nature of ethnicity, sociologists have underestimated the power of the primordial human need to belong.

(B)   Ethnicity is best defined as a dynamic process that combines cultural components with shared political and economic interests.

(C)   In the United States in the twentieth century, ethnic groups have begun to organize in order to further their political and economic interests.

(D)   Ethnicity in the United States has been significantly changed by the Civil Rights movement.

(E)   The two definitions of ethnicity that have dominated sociologists' discussions are incompatible and should be replaced by an entirely new approach.

The Official Guide for GMAT Review (10th edition), #218
GMAT® questions are the property of the Graduate Management
Admission Council® and are reprinted with its permission.

This is a GENERAL question, so review the Skeletal Sketch. Based on the first paragraph, we can eliminate **(A)** as simply untrue. **(B)** restates the last point in the skull of our sketch. **(C)** summarizes details that might be found in paragraphs two and three. **(D)** clearly pertains only to details found in paragraph three. Answer choice **(E)** can be eliminated because of its use of the extreme phrase **entirely new**. After we have eliminated **(A)**, **(C)**, and **(E)**, we must choose between choices **(B)** and **(D)**, which both seem to be likely candidates.

Using the point system for general questions, we can assign **(B)** 2 points, as it relates to the first paragraph. We can assign **(D)** 2 points also, as it relates to paragraphs two and three. In the event of a tie, we should choose the answer choice that relates to the first paragraph over one that does not.

Indeed, the main idea is often explicitly stated near the end of the first paragraph; therefore, you should be able to find it in the skull of your Skeletal Sketch.

Eliminate answer choices that contain extreme words.

Which of the following statements about the first two definitions of ethnicity discussed in the first paragraph is supported by the passage?

    (A)   One is supported primarily by sociologists, and the other is favored by members of ethnic groups.

    (B)   One emphasizes the political aspects of ethnicity, and the other focuses on the economic aspects.

    (C)   One is the result of analysis of United States populations, and the other is the result of analysis of European populations.

    (D)   One focuses more on the ancestral components of ethnicity than does the other.

    (E)   One focuses more on immigrant groups than does the other.

The Official Guide for GMAT Review (10th edition), #219
GMAT® questions are the property of the Graduate Management Admission Council® and are reprinted with its permission.

You should be able to defend the correct answer choice with 1-2 sentences from the passage.

This is a SPECIFIC question that focuses on information presented in the first paragraph. Thus, it can be answered by reviewing the skull of the Skeletal Sketch. **(A)** is not supportable based on the passage, as the first sentence indicates that sociologists have traditionally supported both theories. We can also eliminate **(B)**, because only part of the answer choice is justifiable (one of the theories does indeed focus on the economic aspects of ethnicity, but the other theory does not emphasize the political aspects). **(C)** is not supported by the passage either; the author does not mention the source of the data from which either theory was drawn. **(E)** is also unsupportable; the first paragraph makes no mention of immigrant groups at all.

Reviewing the two definitions in the skull reveals that the correct answer is **(D)**. We can defend this answer choice with two sentences: (1) **The first emphasizes the primordial and unchanging character of ethnicity**, and (2) **A different conception of ethnicity de-emphasizes the cultural component.** Note that the word **primordial** in the passage is a synonym for the key word **ancestral** in choice **(D)**.

The author of the passage refers to Native American people in the second paragraph in order to provide an example of

  (A)   the ability of membership in groups based on shared ancestry and culture to satisfy an essential human need
  (B)   how ethnic feelings have both motivated and been strengthened by political activity
  (C)   how the Civil Rights movement can help promote solidarity among United States ethnic groups
  (D)   how participation in the political system has helped to improve a group's economic situation
  (E)   the benefits gained from renewed study of ethnic history and culture

The Official Guide for GMAT Review (10th edition), #220

GMAT® questions are the property of the Graduate Management Admission Council® and are reprinted with its permission.

> You must be able to justify every word in the correct answer choice.

This is a SPECIFIC question referring to Native Americans. If the question had not helped us by referring to the second paragraph, we could have used our Skeletal Sketch as a search tool and seen that the second paragraph discusses **Native Americans**. The correct answer is **(B)**, which correctly summarizes the interplay between ethnic belonging and political activity described in the passage. We can defend the choice with the following sentence: **Besides leading Native Americans to participate more actively in politics. . . this movement also evoked increased interest in tribal history and traditional culture.**

Note that every word in answer choice **(B)** is justifiable, whereas the other answer choices all contain unjustifiable words. In answer choice **(A)**, there is mention of **an essential human need**. The second paragraph contains no reference to this unnamed need; therefore, the answer choice is not justifiable unless we assume that participation in the political system is an essential human need. (This is clearly too much of an assumption to make on the GMAT.) **(C)** refers to an effect of the Civil Rights movement. Since the Civil Rights movement is mentioned only as a time reference, this answer choice is unjustifiable as well. The word **economic** in answer choice **(D)** is unjustifiable, as the second paragraph contains no reference to the economic situation of the Native Americans. Finally, the word **study** in **(E)** is unjustifiable, since there is no mention of **study** in the second paragraph at all.

The passage supports which of the following statements about the Mexican American community?

(A)   In the 1960's the Mexican American community began to incorporate the customs of another ethnic group in the United States into the observation of its own ethnic holidays.

(B)   In the 1960's Mexican American community groups promoted ethnic solidarity primarily in order to effect economic change.

(C)   In the 1960's leaders of the Mexican American community concentrated their efforts on promoting a renaissance of ethnic history and culture.

(D)   In the 1960's members of the Mexican American community were becoming increasingly concerned about the issue of voting rights.

(E)   In the 1960's the Mexican American community had greater success in mobilizing constituents than did other ethnic groups in the United States.

The Official Guide for GMAT Review (10th edition), #221
GMAT® questions are the property of the Graduate Management
Admission Council® and are reprinted with its permission.

Key words in your sketch will direct you to the relevant paragraph for each specific question.

This is a SPECIFIC question referring to the Mexican American community. Using our Skeletal Sketch as a search tool points us to the third paragraph, which contains the key words **voting rights**. Looking back in the third paragraph reveals that **(D)** is the correct answer.

Again, we can eliminate the other answer choices based on unjustifiable elements. **(A)** can be eliminated based on the word **incorporate**. While the passage does *compare* the customs of Mexican Americans to those of Irish Americans, it does not say anything about one group incorporating the traditions of the other. **(B)** can be eliminated based on the word **economic**. The ethnic solidarity described was primarily concerned with effecting *political* change. **(C)** can be eliminated based on the phrase **renaissance of ethnic history and culture**. Again, the efforts of the Mexican American leaders were concentrated on political action. Finally, **(E)** can be eliminated based on the phrase **other ethnic groups in the United States**. The author makes no comparison between the Mexican American community's success in mobilizing constituents and the success of any other ethnic group in the United States.

Which of the following types of ethnic cultural expression is discussed in the passage?

(A)   The retelling of traditional narratives
(B)   The wearing of traditional clothing
(C)   The playing of traditional music
(D)   The celebration of traditional holidays
(E)   The preparation of traditional cuisine

The Official Guide for GMAT Review (10th edition), #222
GMAT® questions are the property of the Graduate Management
Admission Council® and are reprinted with its permission.

> If you cannot find a particular key word from the question in the passage, look for a synonym.

This is a SPECIFIC question. By scanning the answer choices and reviewing our Skeletal Sketch, we see that only traditional holidays are mentioned in the passage. Looking back in the third paragraph confirms that **(D)** is the correct answer. All the other answer choices can be eliminated quickly based on the fact that they are not mentioned in the passage at all.

Information in the passage supports which of the following statements about many European ethnic groups in the nineteenth-century United States?

(A)   They emphasized economic interests as a way of mobilizing constituents behind certain issues.
(B)   They conceived of their own ethnicity as being primordial in nature.
(C)   They created cultural traditions that fused United States symbols with those of their countries of origin.
(D)   They de-emphasized the cultural components of their communities in favor of political interests.
(E)   They organized formal community groups designed to promote a renaissance of ethnic history and culture.

The Official Guide for GMAT Review (10th edition), #223
GMAT® questions are the property of the Graduate Management
Admission Council® and are reprinted with its permission.

This is a SPECIFIC question referring to European ethnic groups. Using our Skeletal Sketch points us to the key word **Europeans** in the third paragraph. Looking back in the third paragraph reveals that **(C)** is the correct answer. We can defend this answer with the following sentence: **Like European ethnic groups in the nineteenth-century United States, late twentieth-century Mexican American leaders combined ethnic with contemporary civic symbols.** You can consider the word **ethnic** in the passage a synonym for the phrase **those of their countries of origin** in the answer choice, and the word **civic** in the passage a synonym for the phrase **United States symbols** in the answer choice.

The passage suggests that in 1968 Henry Cisneros most likely believed that

  (A) many Mexican Americans would respond positively to the example of Benito Juarez
  (B) many Mexican Americans were insufficiently educated in Mexican history
  (C) the fight for civil rights in the United States had many strong parallels in both Mexican and Irish history
  (D) the quickest way of organizing community-based groups was to emulate the tactics of Benito Juarez
  (E) Mexican Americans should emulate the strategies of Native American political leaders

The Official Guide for GMAT Review (10th edition), #224

GMAT® questions are the property of the Graduate Management Admission Council® and are reprinted with its permission.

This is a SPECIFIC question referring to Henry Cisneros. Using our Skeletal Sketch as a search tool points us to the key word **Cisneros** in the third paragraph. The only sentence that mentions Henry Cisneros reads: **In 1968 Henry Cisneros, later mayor of San Antonio, Texas, cited Mexican leader Benito Juarez as a model for Mexican Americans in their fight for contemporary civil rights.** In this question, you are asked to make an inference. Recall that you want to avoid inferring too much; in fact, you should try to infer as little as possible. Eliminate **(C)** and **(E)** right away, since they contain references to other ethnic groups not mentioned in this sentence at all. Eliminate **(B)** as well, since it requires us to ascribe motives to Cisneros that are possible, but unsupported by the passage. Then eliminate **(D)**, because the phrase **community-based groups** is unjustifiable.

(A) is the correct answer; it simply states that **many** (but not all) Mexican Americans would respond positively. Note that it also uses the noncommittal word **example**, which is much more general than the unjustifiable **tactics** in answer choice **(D)**.

As you can tell from the preceding questions, the Skeletal Sketch is an invaluable tool for answering Reading Comprehension questions about LONG passages. The Sketch provides ready-made answers to GENERAL questions, saving you time spent looking back in the passage. Additionally, the Sketch acts as an ideal search tool to locate answers to SPECIFIC questions, saving you time spent rereading or re-scanning the entire passage.

Now try using our Skeletal Sketch from **Passage 2** to answer REAL GMAT questions about this LONG passage. You can find this passage and the accompanying questions on pages 44-45 of *The Official Guide for GMAT Verbal Review*. Be sure to first identify each question as either GENERAL or SPECIFIC, and use the Skeletal Sketch accordingly. You can check your answers by looking at the explanations in *The Official Guide for Verbal Review*.

When answering inference questions, be careful not to infer too much.

Please refer back to the previous section or to *The Official Guide for GMAT Review, 11th Edition* (pages 370-371) in order to reread **Passage 3**. Here is the DETAIL MAP that we created for this SHORT passage:

<u>Researchers: electroreceptors at tip of anteater's snout</u>
→ Discovery: Exposed small parts of snout to weak electric fields + recorded brain activity
→ Tactile receptors on snout only respond to stronger fields

<u>Investigation: How anteaters utilize electroreceptors</u>
→ Experiment: trained to distinguish water troughs by electric field
→ Hypothesis: use receptors to detect signals given off by prey
→ No signals detected yet from termites, though anteaters locate them very quickly

Use your Detail Map to help you answer questions.

According to the passage, which of the following is a characteristic that distinguishes electroreceptors from tactile receptors?

    (A)   The manner in which electroreceptors respond to electrical stimuli
    (B)   The tendency of electroreceptors to be found in clusters
    (C)   The unusual locations in which electroreceptors are found in most species
    (D)   The amount of electrical stimulation required to excite electroreceptors
    (E)   The amount of nervous activity transmitted to the brain by electroreceptors when they are excited

The Official Guide for GMAT Review (11th edition), #64
GMAT® questions are the property of the Graduate Management
Admission Council® and are reprinted with its permission.

This is a SPECIFIC question. Looking in our Detail Map for **tactile receptors** reveals that the correct answer is **(D)**. This answer choice can be defended by the following sentence: **Tactile receptors . . . do so only in response to electrical field strengths about 1,000 times greater than those known to excite electroreceptors.**

Which of the following can be inferred about the experiment described in the first paragraph?

(A)   Researchers had difficulty verifying the existence of electroreceptors in the anteater because electroreceptors respond to such a narrow range of electrical field strengths.

(B)   Researchers found that the level of nervous activity in the anteater's brain increased dramatically as the strength of the electrical stimulus was increased.

(C)   Researchers found that some areas of the anteater's snout were not sensitive to a weak electrical stimulus.

(D)   Researchers found that the anteater's tactile receptors were more easily excited by a strong electrical stimulus than were the electroreceptors.

(E)   Researchers tested small areas of the anteater's snout in order to ensure that only electroreceptors were responding to the stimulus.

The Official Guide for GMAT Review (11th edition), #65
GMAT® questions are the property of the Graduate Management
Admission Council® and are reprinted with its permission.

Even though an inference is not stated in the passage, you should still be able to defend it with 1-2 sentences from the passage.

This is a SPECIFIC question regarding the first paragraph. Also note that this is a GMAT inference question, which means that the answer should be a fairly obvious deduction. Looking at our Detail Map reveals that **(C)** is the only plausible answer: since the researchers located the electroreceptors on only small parts of the anteater's snout (at the tip), obviously some areas of the anteater's snout do not contain electroreceptors. This answer choice can be defended by the following sentence: **The researchers made this discovery by exposing small areas of the snout to extremely weak electrical fields and recording the transmission of resulting nervous activity to the brain.**

The author of the passage most probably discusses the function of tactile receptors in order to

(A)   eliminate an alternative explanation of anteaters' response to electrical stimuli

(B)   highlight a type of sensory organ that has a function identical to that of electroreceptors

(C)   point out a serious complication in the research on electroreceptors in anteaters

(D)   suggest that tactile receptors assist electroreceptors in the detection of electrical signals

(E)   introduce a factor that was not addressed in the research on electroreceptors in anteaters

The Official Guide for GMAT Review (11th edition), #66

GMAT® questions are the property of the Graduate Management
Admission Council® and are reprinted with its permission.

Eliminate answer
choices if there is no
evidence to support
them in the passage.

This is a SPECIFIC question regarding the function of tactile receptors. Looking at the location of **tactile receptors** in our Detail Map reveals that it appears in the first paragraph, in the following sentence: **While it is true that tactile receptors, another kind of sensory organ on the anteater's snout, can also respond to electrical stimuli, such receptors do so only in response to electrical field strengths about 1,000 times greater than those known to excite electroreceptors.** As tactile receptors are presented in contrast to electroreceptors, you can eliminate **(B)** and **(D)**. There is no evidence to support **(C)** or **(E)**. The sentence's function is to counter a potential objection to the electroreceptor discovery. Thus, **(A)** is the correct answer.

Which of the following can be inferred about anteaters from the behavioral experiment mentioned in the second paragraph?

(A)   They are unable to distinguish between stimuli detected by their electroreceptors and stimuli detected by their tactile receptors.
(B)   They are unable to distinguish between the electrical signals emanating from termite mounds and those emanating from ant nests.
(C)   They can be trained to recognize consistently the presence of a particular stimulus.
(D)   They react more readily to strong than to weak stimuli.
(E)   They are more efficient at detecting stimuli in a controlled environment than in a natural environment.

The Official Guide for GMAT Review (11ᵗʰ edition), #67
GMAT® questions are the property of the Graduate Management
Admission Council® and are reprinted with its permission.

Even one word is sometimes enough to make an answer choice unjustifiable.

This is a SPECIFIC question regarding the experiment in the second paragraph. Also note that this is a GMAT inference question, which means that the answer should be a fairly obvious deduction. **(A)** is unjustifiable because of the phrase **tactile receptors**, which are not mentioned in the second paragraph at all. **(B)** is unjustifiable because of the words **ant nests**, which are mentioned in the passage but are never compared to termite mounds in any way. **(D)** is unjustifiable because of the word **strong**, which is not mentioned in the passage, and **(E)** is unjustifiable because of the words **controlled** and **natural**; the passage makes no distinction between the two. Only **(C)** is a logical inference: since the experiment involved training anteaters to distinguish water troughs by electric field, it is clear that the anteaters can be trained to recognize a particular stimulus.

The passage suggests that the researchers mentioned in the second paragraph who observed anteaters break into a nest of ants would most likely agree with which of the following statements?

    (A)   The event they observed provides conclusive evidence that anteaters use their electroreceptors to locate unseen prey.

    (B)   The event they observed was atypical and may not reflect the usual hunting practices of anteaters.

    (C)   It is likely that the anteaters located the ants' nesting chambers without the assistance of electroreceptors.

    (D)   Anteaters possess a very simple sensory system for use in locating prey.

    (E)   The speed with which the anteaters located their prey is greater than what might be expected on the basis of chance alone.

> *The Official Guide for GMAT Review (11th edition), #68*
> GMAT® questions are the property of the Graduate Management
> Admission Council® and are reprinted with its permission.

Making inferences uses many of the same thinking skills as making assumptions.

This is a SPECIFIC question regarding the second paragraph. It asks for an inference, so the answer should be something that can be deduced fairly easily. Look back at the sentences that refer to researchers' observations of anteaters breaking into nests of ants: **Still, researchers have observed anteaters breaking into a nest of ants at an oblique angle and quickly locating nesting chambers. This ability to quickly locate unseen prey suggests, according to the researchers, that the anteaters were using their electroreceptors to locate the nesting chambers.** These two sentences are structured like a Critical Reasoning argument: the first one is a premise and the second is a conclusion. Only **(E)** provides the hidden assumption, that the anteaters' speed (indicated by the word **quickly**) is enough to justify the conclusion.

Which of the following, if true, would most strengthen the hypothesis mentioned in the middle of the second paragraph?

    (A)   Researchers are able to train anteaters to break into an underground chamber that is emitting a strong electrical signal.

    (B)   Researchers are able to detect a weak electrical signal emanating from the nesting chamber of an ant colony.

    (C)   Anteaters are observed taking increasingly longer amounts of time to locate the nesting chambers of ants.

    (D)   Anteaters are observed using various angles to break into nests of ants.

    (E)   Anteaters are observed using the same angle used with nests of ants to break into the nests of other types of prey.

The Official Guide for GMAT Review (11th edition), #69
GMAT® questions are the property of the Graduate Management
Admission Council® and are reprinted with its permission.

> Strengthening a hypothesis is just like strengthening a conclusion.

This is a SPECIFIC question relating to the hypothesis in the second paragraph. Like the previous question, it is similar to a Critical Reasoning question. This time, you are being asked to strengthen the conclusion. Therefore, you should begin by eliminating any answer choices that do not support the conclusion, or hypothesis, mentioned in the line: **anteaters use electroreceptors to detect electrical signals given off by prey**. Eliminate **(C)**, **(D)**, and **(E)**, since they do not support this conclusion. This leaves **(A)** and **(B)**. **(B)** is the better answer because it provides a missing premise. The experiment provides evidence that anteaters can detect weak electrical signals. It also provides evidence that anteaters can quickly locate ant nests. In order to establish a strong relationship between these two facts, we would need evidence that the ant nests do indeed have some electrical signal. Note that **(A)** is also unjustifiable because of the word **train**. If anteaters are *trained* to locate a chamber by using their electroreceptors, this would not provide evidence that they do so naturally to find prey.

As you can tell from the preceding questions, the DETAIL MAP is an invaluable tool for answering Reading Comprehension questions about SHORT passages. The Map provides ready-made answers to almost all questions (both GENERAL and SPECIFIC), saving you time spent looking back in the passage.

Now try using our Detail Map from **Passage 4** to answer REAL GMAT questions about this SHORT passage. You can find this passage and the accompanying questions on pages 354-355 of *The Official Guide for GMAT Review, 11th Edition*. Try to use the Detail Map to answer all of the questions. You can check your answers by looking at the explanations in *The Official Guide for GMAT Review, 11th Edition*.

Reading Comprehension

from *The Official Guide for GMAT Review, 11th Edition* (pages 26-31 & 346-393) and *The Official Guide for GMAT Verbal Review* (pages 22-56)

Read each passage in the Reading Comprehension section of *The Official Guide for GMAT Review, 11th Edition* and *The Official Guide for GMAT Verbal Review*, and answer all questions.

Before you read each passage, identify whether it is LONG or SHORT. (Note that the line lengths are slightly different than those on a computer screen, so the long-short line count cutoff is different. LONG passages are those with more than 35 lines. SHORT passages are those with 35 lines or less.)

As you read the passage, create a Skeletal Sketch (for LONG passages) or a Detail Map (for SHORT passages). You should preview the first question before reading, but do not look at any of the subsequent questions prior to reading the passage, since you will not be able to do this on the CAT.

Then, use your Skeletal Sketch or Detail Map to assist you in answering all the questions that accompany the passage.

Use the following formula for timing guidelines:

(# of questions on passage) $\times$ 2 = total # of minutes you should spend
(including reading and answering questions)

For example, if there are 4 questions for a given passage, you should spend eight minutes in total doing all the work for that passage. As a rule of thumb, spend a little less than half the allotted time reading, skimming, and sketching, and a little more than half the time answering questions. In this example, you would spend 3 to 3.5 minutes reading and sketching, and 4.5 to 5 minutes answering the questions.

Finally, a GMAT* prep guide series that goes beyond the basics.

Word Translations ISBN: 0-9748069-2-7 Retail: $26

Critical Reasoning & Reading Comprehension
ISBN: 0-9748069-6-x
Retail: $26

Number Properties
ISBN: 0-9748069-0-0
Retail: $26

Geometry
ISBN: 0-9748069-4-3
Retail: $26

Equations, Inequalities & VIC's
ISBN: 0-9748069-3-5
Retail: $26

Sentence Correction
ISBN: 0-9748069-5-1
Retail: $26

Fractions, Decimals, & Percents
ISBN: 0-9748069-1-9
Retail: $26

Published by

Manhattan **GMAT** *Prep*

You get many more pages per topic than found in all-in-one tomes.

Only buy those guides that address the specific skills you need to develop.

Gain access to Online Practice GMAT* Exams & bonus question banks.

COMMENTS FROM GMAT TEST TAKERS:

Now Available at your local bookstore!

"Bravo, Manhattan GMAT! Bravo! The 7 guides truly did not disappoint. All the guides are clear, concise, and well organized and explained things in a manner that made it possible to understand things the first time through without missing any of the important details."

"I've thumbed through a lot of books that don't even touch these. The fact that they're split up into components is immeasurably helpful. The set-up of each guide and the lists of past GMAT problems make for an incredibly thorough and easy to follow study path."

*GMAT and GMAC are registered trademarks of the Graduate Management Admission Council which neither sponsors nor endorses this product.